Cracking
the
College
Code

*A practical guide to making the most of
the first year college experience*

Catherine O'Connor

ORIGINAL WRITING

The information contained in this book does not relate to any one course or third level college in particular but can be taken as a general guide for all. Each college sets out its own specific rules and regulations and it is the responsibility of each student to familiarise himself/herself with these rules.

The terms 'parent' and 'parents' are used widely in this book and can be taken to include 'guardian' or 'guardians' in all contexts.

ISBNS
Parent : 978-1-78237-357-5
epub: 978-1-78237-358-2
mobi: 978-1-78237-359-9
PDF: 978-1-78237-360-5

A cip catalogue for this book is available from the National Library.

Published by Original Writing Ltd., Dublin, 2013.

Printed by Clondalkin Group, Glasnevin, Dublin 11

Tempus fugit

"A brilliant book and what every student, parent/guardian needs to read on entry to third level education. Informative, realistic and comprehensive. This book kept me interested every step of the way. Superbly written and something I will refer to time and time again."

Nora Irwin: Parent and former Director, National Parents Council Post Primary and Executive Committee Member, COMPASS (Co-operation of Minority Religions & Protestant Parents Association)

"Cracking the College Code has a wealth of information for both aspiring and current third level students and their parents alike. It is very accessible, well researched and comprehensive. It gives a valuable insight into how the college system really works - a wonderful resource."

Dr Veronica O'Dwyer: Lecturer of Optometry, Dublin Institute of Technology

"I wish this book was around when I was starting out. It opens prospective students' minds to everything you don't think of about third level. A must-read for anyone thinking about going to college."

Jenny Stokes: A recent college graduate

"This book has a broad appeal and is a timely and practical guide for both students and parents. It will guide students through their first year at college exploring a world where independent learning is not just encouraged but expected. It will provide parents with an insight into how the system works and the challenges faced by first year students, challenges which can often overwhelm. It will be of interest to guidance counsellors and those working with sixth years as they prepare students to make a smooth transition between two very different systems. Worthwhile, realistic and practical, it will be of immense value to students, parents and student support staff."

Robert Dunne: Principal, Loreto Abbey Secondary School, Dalkey, Co Dublin

"Any book with the capacity to enhance an individual's experience of college and simultaneously improve their education and professional development has to be welcomed by students and parents alike. There is no secret method or magic formula, just a direct and pragmatic introduction to college life and a set of guidelines for making the transition from second level efficiently, effectively and quickly. The book accomplishes this with warmth, integrity and common sense.

It will also be welcomed by policy makers, leaders and professional educators who will see students prepared to engage more speedily with the challenges, facilities and benefits not to mention privileges that a college education can bring. Employers and professional bodies will also welcome the fact that more effective and creative graduates will become available to sustain the growth, well-being and success of a nation. The small incremental effect of a book like this in the hands of students and their parents, could contribute greatly to many professional careers and lives and hence to society.

Catherine O'Connor is eminently qualified in terms of her achievements within all the main aspects of the academic world, research, teaching, pastoral care and management. Add to that, her own business experience, both self-employed and across many organisations. Also add, her hands-on experience as a parent and finally her absolute passion for education and you have the author of this book."

Alan Mullally, former Director of I.S. programmes and elected member of Council at Trinity College Dublin, following a series of senior management roles and directorships in industry. He has served as external examiner at many third level colleges and continues his commitment to education through Oscail, Dublin City University.

CONTENTS

Acknowledgements

I would like to thank all who assisted me in writing this book.

To the many students, parents, teachers, guidance counsellors and school principals who offered opinion and much debate on the many issues addressed.

To my colleagues and friends at Trinity College Dublin, in particular those at the School of Computer Science and Statistics. To my associates at Dublin City University, University College Dublin, University College Cork, University College Galway, the National University of Ireland, Maynooth, University of Limerick, Dublin Institute of Technology and all other Institutes of Technology, the Department of Education and Skills, the Higher Education Authority of Ireland, the Institute of Guidance Counsellors, the National Parents Council Post Primary, other government agencies and contributors that have the education of our young people at heart.

A special thanks to Alan Mullally for his support and encouragement over many years.

To my son James and daughter Katie, who were the inspiration for this book, and to their many college friends who were persuaded to interview at my kitchen table.

To my close family and friends, impossible to thank each one individually but you know who you are.

Most of all my greatest thanks to my husband Tim who is always by my side.

INTRODUCTION

This book is written to inform students and parents about making a successful transition from second level to third level and about meeting the many challenges faced in this process.

It is a practical hands-on guide about the challenges faced in moving from the relatively rigid structures imposed at second level to an environment where the learning becomes self-directed and where the student takes responsibility for the learning activities around a chosen course.

The information does not relate to any one course or college in particular but can be taken as a general guide of what to expect on almost every course and at all levels whether degree, diploma or certificate.

It highlights the significant differences between two distinct levels within the education system as students prepare to make a move from dependence on teachers, parents and school to independent learning. It should give a quiet confidence to parents to let go and to students to take control, having identified and maybe even discussed some of these challenging differences together.

You should come away with lots of information, insights and tips to assist in what is a most exciting journey of great discovery and the stepping stone to a lifetime of work and leisure in an unpredictable, evolving and demanding world.

Catherine O'Connor

Chapter 1

SETTING THE SCENE

Welcome to Cracking the College Code, a practical guide to help you to make a smooth transition from second level to third level. You are now probably at one of two stages.

You may be in the final cycle of second level education and have mixed opinions about what you should do after your Leaving Certificate. You have decisions to make and many hurdles to climb. If you are planning to go to college, this book will give you a good understanding of what third level is about, what to expect and ways to manage the transition from second level effectively.

If you are already in your first year of college, you may be looking for guidance and you will find lots of information in this book to help you manage the various challenges as they are presented to you over the academic year. First, let's look at some facts about Ireland's participation rates in higher education today.

Approximately two thirds of our second level student population enter higher education. This figure stood at approximately 20% in 1980.

According to the Higher Education Authority of Ireland (HEA), the body governing our publicly funded third level institutions, more than one-third of the Irish population (25-64 years) hold a higher education qualification and 45% of those between the ages of 25 and 34 hold such a qualification.

Our higher level participation rates stand proudly alongside that of our EU counterparts and according to the National Strategy for Higher Education 2030 Report; all the indications suggest that these participation rates will continue to rise in the coming years.

This is positive news for Ireland. However, such participation brings stronger competition which can also mean a greater struggle for many of you entering the third level system as you try to cope with the pressure to achieve academically. For this reason, there is a need to understand this system and how to work it to best advantage.

To do this we need to see the situation from two different perspectives, that of the parent and that of the student.

The parent perspective

Some years ago, your parents were handed you, a little bundle of joy, without a manual or a 'to do' list. Very soon they realised that this bundle of joy was quite unique with a distinct little personality, an independent mind and a complete identity which was not exactly described in any text book.

In the intervening years, they may have been handed further bundles of joy and again and again these personalities presented quite differently, each with a unique identity. They probably gave little thought to the challenges ahead and perhaps that wasn't a bad thing because if they knew then what they know now, they might have spent too long trying to work things out instead of getting on with the real job of parenting.

They may have picked up bits of advice from their parents, grandparents, relatives or friends and any other willing voice or helping hand on the way. Many of them have faced and continue to face the challenges alone, far away from the influences of family and friends, some by choice and others by necessity.

Parents worry, some more than others. Most will readily admit that the worry of an unhappy or an unwell child is the greatest burden of all. The bond between child and parent, whether good or bad, is a lifetime connection. It is in the interest of maintaining and developing this lifetime connection that parents try to guide your pathway in life.

No matter what their personal circumstances, they have learned to meet the challenges presented so far which have come in different guises and situations, sometimes filled with a mixture of feelings and emotions, some good, some not so good. The challenges have been different through the many stages of your development, from the infant to the adolescent.

This book concerns itself with yet another one of life's challenges, the subject of how parents can work with you to help you to prepare for a smooth transition from second level to third level and make that first year college experience a success. You are their future, their hope, their hearts and their lives. Along the way, you challenge them as in turn they try to nurture and value you by facilitating your growth and development making you contributing citizens of a shared future.

Your generation was born into a society of economic boom, growing up in a world where the supermarket never closes, social networking operates around the clock, Christmas presents never come in ones, birthdays are celebrated twice over, landlines are foreign, the Internet and smart phones are a necessity, collections from school are routine, walking is an exercise rather than a mode of transport, fast food is commonplace and family gatherings around the table at mealtimes are often limited.

Your generation of parents tried to achieve it all:

> To work
> To travel
> To play
> To entertain
> To be entertained
> To communicate
> To love unconditionally
> To spoil
> To endear
> To please

> To accommodate
> To spare hardship
> To provide comforts
> To solve problems
> To do everything and be everything for their children
> To do things one step better than the generation before

The transition from boom to bust has been quick and painful. All families have been affected, regardless of position or level of income. Adapting quickly from prosperity to austerity can be a difficult and challenging task.

The task of moving from the more pre-determined structure at second level to a self-directed learning environment at third level can also be a difficult and challenging task. This move requires a shift from the highly interdependent learning path at second level where teachers, students and parents have worked together for many years in determining your daily life and routines.

A big challenge lies with parents as they try to let go and come to terms with the fact that you have to do this on your own in order to succeed. While it is your responsibility to manage this transition successfully, parents can help you by understanding and maybe discussing some of the many challenges faced in this process.

Enrolling on a course of study may happen at the stroke of a pen but completing a course of study is an entirely separate matter. Third level is about education in the broadest and most complete sense of the word encompassing personal, social and professional development.

The student perspective

You, the student, are the most important person in this book.

Up to now, most decisions regarding your education have been taken by other people, usually your parent/s. Some of these decisions you were happy about, some not. But you went along with most of them, put up with the consequences and tried to make the most of the experience.

Now you have been thrown into a period of uncertainty where the decision-making process is dramatically changing and the dependable fixed structures of your path in education to date are about to change forever. You are expected to make big decisions about the what, why, when and where you are going to study for the next three to four years.

This time it is all about you. This is about your life. It is your opportunity. It may only come once. It is a time to start over, to discover new things, to make mistakes, to make new friends, to leave school life behind. It is a dream waiting to be delivered.

5

Above all, it is a costly process, requiring a massive economic and social investment with a substantial price tag. It is only right that such a big decision gets due attention and research.

This book will address the following and more, relating to your first year college experience:

> Choosing a course which best fits you
> Why college is so different from second level
> How the communication channels work
> Day to day life in college
> Making the best use of college services
> Understanding the examination process
> Becoming an independent learner and a successful student
> Living at home with family or away with fellow students
> How to make college a fun and enjoyable experience
> Meeting expectations

It sets out to help you to make the most of that first year college experience. In doing so, it can lay the foundation for your entire time in college and contribute hugely to your development in future life.

Making a good choice in your study path is key to having a positive first year college experience.

Chapter 2 gives some useful steps that you can follow in trying to find the course of study and the college that suits you best.

Chapter 2

CHOOSING YOUR STUDY PATH

It is internationally recognised that making a poor course choice is one of the main reasons why students withdraw from courses during or after the first year of college. Some students know quite quickly that they have made a poor decision, however, for others it can be a gradual dawning only coming to light towards the end of the first year.

You may find the first few weeks of college difficult for a variety of reasons and initially feel that you have made a poor choice of course. This feeling may pass as you may also slowly discover that it can take some time to become familiar with the course content and to grasp the fundamental concepts under discussion, all delivered within a very different education system. Take time to read in detail about these differences in chapter 3 and about day to day life at college in chapter 4.

Students who make poor choices see college as one big struggle in their first year and being unaware of what they should expect on entering the system, they can assume that this experience is normal and keep those feelings to themselves. That feeling of being under pressure starts to creep in, a pressure which is added to by the associated academic demands from a course that they do not really like or enjoy.

In this chapter we will look at steps that you might take in trying to find a course that suits you. Finding what interests you is the first step. Once this interest is harnessed, then the work begins on finding the courses close to this interest and a college that suits your individual needs best.

Choosing your study path takes time and requires hard work, determination, tenacity and patience. There is usually at least one course that is a best fit or match for every student. Finding this best fit is the starting point in making a successful transition to third level.

Some of the mixed feelings and anxieties of students prior to entry to college and in the first few weeks at college are reflected below:

By now you may have spotted the following:

"Oh no, I didn't think I'd get this course – it's not for me"

What this tells us is that the course offered was probably not listed as a genuine preference and that not enough effort was put into researching this course and all other courses listed in the application.

In depth research and consultation prior to choosing a course of study will significantly reduce the chances of this happening to you.

Imagine if you were given a blank cheque to travel around the world in one direction only, stopping off for one year at a time in three or four different countries. How do you think you might approach such an adventure? I am guessing that you might visit many websites, consult with travel experts and many others considering matters such as:

› Climate
› Safety
› Access
› Economy
› Political order/disorder
› Human rights
› Cultural differences
› Language
› War
› Crime
› Health and healthcare facilities
› Education

The list is endless.

The depth of enquiry in choosing your study path is also endless. This depth of enquiry is required for all courses you have listed in your CAO application.

Having already discussed how poor course choice is one of the main reasons for withdrawing from college, we need to establish and understand other reasons why some students withdraw. We can then look at what steps can be taken to avoid such a withdrawal. Given current economic challenges and the rising participation rates at third level, this is more important than ever.

Withdrawal from courses means financial loss, a loss that has to be picked up by you, a parent, the state, or all three.

WHY STUDENTS WITHDRAW FROM COURSES

Social difficulties
Adapting socially into the new college environment is key to both social and academic development. Friends are very important in student life and help shape the college experience. The challenge of moving from the old school network to making new friends at college can be liberating for some but daunting for others.

There are many opportunities which can help you to make an easy social integration at college. These include joining societies and clubs which can be associated with both leisure interests and academic pursuits. These and other opportunities are discussed in chapter 7, Making use of the college services.

Academic performance
The transition to third level is a steep learning curve. Fear of poor academic performance can be a worry to the new student. The move from a structured, dependent approach at second level to a world of self-directed independent learning is difficult.

At college, you will learn in different environments where different styles and approaches in teaching and learning are adopted with the move away from learning by rote to an emphasis on understanding and critical thinking.

You will have to manage time and conflicting workloads, work in groups, learn to write in a particular academic style and master new terminology. It is important to know that you are not alone in this and that there is help available, often locally within your department or through the wider college services. Recognise when you need to seek help and how to set about proactively engaging with the services at such times, see chapter 7.

Study commitment
Some students enter college with little understanding of the level of study required in order to achieve academically. You will need a strong study ethos. You need to commit to a demanding academic workload and take full responsibility for your learning journey.

At third level the pace is faster than you are used to at second level. The level of enquiry is different, the study load is greater and more challenging as many other demands are placed on you which can interfere with giving such commitment.

Financial worries
The rising costs of going to college have to be met. These can include: fees, transport, food, rent, utilities, clothing, books and materials, medical and social costs. Some students depend on grant aid but can often experience long delays in receiving payments. Many also need to work long hours to fund the educational experience often leading to serious time pressures which can conflict with the academic workload and lead to a reduced study commitment. In the current economic climate the problem of finding suitable part-time work can also add to the worries for students.

It is important for you to establish how your education will be financed. See 'Student Finance' in the useful links section on where to find information on financial supports available.

Under-preparedness in subjects

Students who enrol in Science and Mathematics related courses are often unaware of the differences in the study of these subjects at third level.

Courses which demand a higher level entry qualification in Mathematics are geared towards the student who is comfortable with solving problems using underpinning mathematical concepts and techniques. While early lectures in these areas will deal with the fundamentals of the subjects under study, the pace of the lectures moves quickly afterwards. If you are struggling with Mathematics at school, this pattern may continue at college.

However, this should not deter you from pursuing a particular career choice which requires mathematical knowledge and skills. There are many courses, short and long, available to you to develop mathematical ability ranging from face to face to online to distance programmes which meet most requirements. Such courses are also available in many other subjects. A little homework on all can pay dividends.

Most colleges provide additional free support in Mathematics to first year students. Special support services may also be provided in other subjects, for example, Language, Science and Computer Programming. You will need to check your course/college to establish what supports are in place for your chosen course and subjects of study.

Fixation on careers

Sometimes parents can get fixed on the notion that you must follow a set career path, must be somebody, must be something, must do what generations have done or must do what generations haven't done. This is intertwined with the model of the more traditional careers of the graduates of years gone by, not taking into account the advent of an information and digital age in which employers seek out specific sets of skills to fill roles that have yet to be created and defined.

Career paths have changed and movement between jobs and across sectors is not unusual as society seeks to meet social, economic and cultural challenges.

Fixations on career prospects at this early stage of your social and academic development can become an additional unwanted pressure.

FINDING THE BEST FIT COURSE FOR YOU

Choosing the best fit course is of vital importance. To achieve this best fit requires your serious thought and engagement. It is also advisable to work with the guidance counsellor at your school who can provide information on the many courses and services available at the different colleges.

The Central Applications Office (CAO) system

The purpose of the CAO system is to handle the administrative function of allocating places to students entering undergraduate courses in the third level system. It is a system that requires students to place courses in order of choice on a list. By process of elimination through the allocation of points, places are offered primarily based on demand.

The CAO system is a tool. While points will ultimately dictate an offer of a place on a course at a particular date in time, points do not govern wants, wishes, interests and personal choices. It is most important that you choose courses in order of your genuine interest.

If you are set on studying a course attracting very high points, then you must think about what other routes you can take to get to a similar place:

> Are there related courses which might be of equal interest?
> Are there colleges further afield offering the same or similar courses with different entry requirements?

When the CAO application is submitted early in the academic year of entry to the system, it serves two functions. It completes the formal registration process and gives you some focus in thinking about course choices. As you are reading this, you may be reasonably focused and that's great. If you don't have that focus, you should be reassured in the knowledge that your choices can be changed subsequent to that first registration towards the end of the Leaving Certificate cycle.

Don't think about the CAO as being only about points. It's about choosing the right study path for you taking into account your interests, wants and choices. If you have a genuine interest in what you study at third level, you are more likely to succeed.

More than one course

Students often fall into the trap of placing only one course of interest on the CAO application. Placing one course of interest is not to be recommended. While general predictions can be made, external factors come into play and points awarded may fall short thus eliminating an offer of any course to study.

You need to have a selection of courses. If only one course of interest is placed on the form and the points don't match, then you will be left with no options. Your search should be wide to start. Whether you are generally interested in Psychology, Mathematics, Business, Engineering, Arts or Medicine, you must work towards defining a more focused interest. Once this is established you need to seek out courses within that area of interest which you can realistically pursue at third level.

It is also most useful to explore all colleges offering similar courses. This includes local, national and international searches. Such searches can reveal new insights into your area of interest and uncover other courses related to this interest.

It's not about pleasing family and friends

This is and should be your decision. Family and friends can and will positively influence your decisions but sometimes traditions and experiences in families can be imposed as you try to break free and follow your own dream.

The path of study you follow may or may not fit in with the family plans but the path of study is not about the family. It is all about you; you are the most important decision maker in all of this process.

Academic snobbery

As a nation, we are full of it. How many times have we encountered parents who insist on spreading the word about the number of points achieved? Some parents feel the need to broadcast to the world about how academic/intellectual/non-academic their sons or daughters are.

There is also competition within families, between families, between city/town and country. We hear "my son/daughter is very bright; he/she just doesn't do well in exams." We also hear "if they spent as much time on their study as they do on those devices, they would be geniuses." Some families suffer more than others from this. The question of students wasting excess points gained in the Leaving Certificate, maybe studying Arts instead of Medicine, Business instead of Law can be irritating to some parents.

Some families have students who achieve very high grades and others who under-achieve. Whichever end of the spectrum you land, that is where you are and I suspect that if you are reading this book you are looking to make the most of the next educational opportunity.

STEPS THAT YOU CAN TAKE TO FIND THE BEST FIT COURSE FOR YOU

Think about the dream course
Everyone must dream, there is no cost in doing so. There is a feel good factor from the process and often these dreams are the seeds of many future endeavours.

So whether in your mind or on paper, you need to dream about studying any course, on any subject, anywhere in the world. Some useful exercises are recommended at the end of this chapter to facilitate this process.

Eliminate what you don't want to do
›   If you hate numbers, why study accountancy?
›   If you faint every single time at the sight of blood or on hospital visits, why study nursing, dentistry or medicine?
›   If you are the last to want to know how and why things work and have no interest in building, designing or fixing things, why choose engineering?
›   If you dislike being around children, why would you teach?

› If you don't like foreign languages, why would you study them at college?

Establish your subject interests
This may come directly from subjects studied at school. What are your favourite subjects and why? Do you demonstrate a natural aptitude for...?

› Figures
› Language
› Science

What about subjects you haven't chosen at school? Given timetabling and resource constraints at second level, students are often precluded from studying subjects of great interest to them.

› What makes you get up early on a Saturday morning?
› What makes you tick?
› Have you an enquiring mind?
› What interests you most in terms of debate and discussion?
› What do you get passionate about?
› How do you express yourself?
› Are you a naturally good writer or a naturally good speaker?
› Who do you look up to and why?

You may have a strong relationship with friends or some family members, often a grandparent, who can unlock many of the keys to these interests. Sometimes, parents have to accept that they may not always be the first to know about some of your interests, a temporary little affront to pride which in time becomes insignificant in the context of the overall pleasure of seeing you develop in life.

Occupational testing

Guidance counsellors at school offer valuable advice with most setting students some formal assessment which may glean subject interest, aptitudes and determine intellectual ability.

Not all testing can be taken as absolute. A more holistic approach is required with multiple factors taken into consideration which may guide your path of study. At different stages, you can work with your guidance counsellor, teachers, parents and others to assist in this process.

Become informed

There will be much opinion expressed by you and other interested parties about different courses. Parents may set out to find information and facts and become desperate to tell you everything. They have your best interest at heart and are also presenting this information from the lens of maturity and life experience which should not be ignored.

You, on the other hand, are the one in the situation and may not take kindly to advice which is sometimes perceived as instruction from an interfering parent. This is quite normal. In other cases, students and parents can also work comfortably together in the process.

To take full control of your learning journey, you will need to work hard. Maybe your parents won't get involved at all or they may stay on the side-line and observe, throwing the odd burst of enthusiasm and encouragement while others may stifle progress by taking on the project of dictating your choice of study path.

Where you have openly expressed a genuine wish to attend third level but are undecided, lacking in confidence and struggling to establish the reasons why you are sitting the Leaving Certificate at all, then your parent may become more involved. More than often in such cases, you may not wish to cooperate with such enquiry. If this is the case, your parent will probably work quietly and independently of you to keep informed.

In the end, it is unimportant who has sought or found the information; the most important matter is that you make an informed choice about your study path.

You may be very proactive and self-directed in your enquiry about studying at third level. This is the ideal situation, however, occasionally you may also think you have uncovered everything you need to know about a particular path of study. When this knowledge is questioned and tested, it may turn out to be at surface level and on entering the third level system with this surface knowledge you may find that your expectations may be mismatched.

Getting below the surface
The interests must first be established. In the early stages, the enquiry will probably be wide incorporating all subject areas. Gradually, through the process of further deliberation and reflection, using any tools made available to you in school and the recommendations and exercises contained within this book, a narrowing of interests should emerge. This, together with any information you may have gleaned from data regarding your aptitude and abilities, begins the process of narrowing your interest areas further.

The Internet is your first port of call. By visiting websites, you can find information relating to the wider course under study, the subjects within that study, the methods of delivery and assessment and the range of career options open following graduation. You also need to find out about the specific subjects taught in the first year of study.

First select the courses of interest. Look at all third level institutions offering these courses, at home and further afield, exploring how each college delivers similar courses and the type of content covered. Information on the individual college websites will bring you to different levels. The level of access and detail presented will vary from college to college and from course to course. Don't be put off by this. Continue in your efforts. You will be surprised by what you can uncover in relation to subjects studied, course content, methods of delivery, lecture hours and much more.

Book lists and/or useful links to handbooks may be available on college/course websites. A good look at the table of contents in the recommended text books in any subject area will arouse further interest or may have the opposite effect. The more you delve at this level the more you can uncover and gain a better understanding of the subject matter in your course choice. This level of research will result in a better match to your expectations of college.

Don't worry if you find one or two of the many subjects taught within your course in the first year unappealing. In all courses of study, every student will find one or two subjects unappealing. However, if you find *most* of the subjects unappealing within your chosen course, then you really have cause for concern and need to conduct more research before making your final choice.

Such detailed research into all courses listed on your CAO application should significantly reduce the risk of making a poor choice.

It is also important to look at the spread of options for study over the lifetime of the college course you choose. Many courses offer specialisations and opportunities to study abroad. You need to consider all of this carefully in terms of both course and college choice.

Making contact with college

Explore opportunities to make contact with the college/s of interest to you. Student intake at third level is now more competitive than ever as colleges seek to get their share of the incoming student population.

You are seen to be a very valuable financial resource to any college as your commitment to attend for three or four years guarantees a steady flow of income. Given your value, it is in the college's interest that you choose the right course of study and more importantly that you 'stay the course' for the allocated time.

Opportunities for making contact with colleges can include:

› The annual Higher Options event
› Regional college/career events
› School career fairs
› Interaction with student ambassadors and academics on Open Days
› Visits by college staff/students to second level schools
› Arranged visits to the college campus
› Scheduled visits to meet lecturers
› Workshop activities
› Shadowing days
› Taster days
› General interactions with college students

You need to lose your inhibitions, use every resource available to you and learn how to extend your network beyond schools, communities, families, neighbours, friends and acquaintances.

In any given neighbourhood, a number of students will be studying courses of similar interest and attending a college of your interest. It is also quite likely that these students will know graduates from these courses who, when contacted, will be delighted to offer insights into their experiences and opportunities arising. So when your parents and/or guidance counsellors encourage you to take advantage of the extended network, remember this network may have useful information regarding study paths and how such study paths might lead to different and exciting careers.

Compile a list of questions you might like answered. This list will change as your direction becomes more focused.

Choosing the right college

Colleges vary in size and structures. Similar courses are on offer in many colleges which suit different students for quite different reasons.

Many things need to be considered when choosing your college including:

> Geographical location
> Financial implications
> Number of students attending the college
> Number of students taking the particular course of study
> Natural student catchment
> Course content
> Methods of teaching
> Academic year structure
> Assessment methods
> College services
> Type and quality of support services
> Disability services
> Sports facilities
> The social scene
> Internship opportunities
> Opportunities to study abroad
> International reputation
> National and local reputation
> Graduate opportunities
> Links with employers and industry

Study abroad

It is important for you to establish if courses have an optional or, more importantly, a compulsory year of study abroad. The latter can be an integral part of many courses offering foreign languages. In these cases, generally the examinations in the exchange university abroad are taken in the foreign language and this can be a challenge.

With some courses, such as Business, it may be possible to attend a college abroad but follow the course of study through English. Where courses offer an optional year of study abroad, students choosing to stay at home for that year may be offered a local industry/research internship instead. This varies from college to college and from course to course.

Regardless of country of study, moving abroad to a new social and cultural environment requires major adjustments and is not for the faint-hearted. It is always good to talk to students who have had this experience. Many things need to be thought through before you make a commitment. These can include:

> › Geographical location
> › Openness to embrace cultural and language differences
> › Financial implications
> › The wider academic and social implications
> › The assessment process

Most students return from this experience older and wiser and much improved in the foreign language. The ability to communicate to a high standard in a foreign language is an enviable skill and once mastered at an early age, can be built upon. Such skill greatly enhances the ability of any graduate to be mobile and employable across the globe.

FEELING UNDECIDED

Simple but useful exercises follow which might generate ideas to assist you if you are still feeling undecided about your choice of study path.

Here's what I am good at	Here's what I need help with

People I admire	Why?

Subjects that interest me in school	Subjects that interest me outside of school

My dream job	My dream place of work

At least one college and one study path will best suit your needs. While the responsibility lies with you to choose the best fit, your parents can also offer support by facilitating this process, working quietly in the background.

We live in a fast moving information and digital age. Many of the jobs of our future have yet to be created. While one course of study may be taken, graduates of today's world will more than likely have a few career paths, many jobs and plenty of future educational opportunities. In time, many of the chosen career paths will seem totally unrelated to the original course of study.

Through the college experience, you will acquire a unique set of transferable skills as each course of study prepares you for the rapidly evolving and changing demands of our unpredictable world. What we can predict at this point is that your working life is set to be a long one. What a dream to find work in an area you might enjoy!

The next chapter addresses the differences between the two systems of second level and third level and details many of the challenges which you may face in moving between these two systems.

Chapter 3

DIFFERENT SYSTEMS: DIFFERENT CHALLENGES

This chapter sets out many of the differences between the second level and third level systems. In this and the following chapters you will identify ways to manage these differences as you prepare to make the transition.

DIFFERENCES BETWEEN SCHOOL AND COLLEGE

School	College
Communication is between student, parent and teachers/ school	*Communication is between student and college*
Deadlines are often flexible with the exception of state examinations	*Deadlines are usually set in stone*
Familiar faces and places	*Unfamiliar faces and places*
Old friends network	*New friends are made*
Students live at home or board	*Students may live at home or live away from home for the first time*
Attendance is compulsory	*Attendance is mostly voluntary*
Study is imposed	*Study is chosen*

School	College
Financial responsibility generally borne by family	Financial responsibility changes and the student is more involved
Formal study periods assigned	No study periods assigned
Teachers and parents often advise study schedules	Students plan their own study schedules
Timetable is set and managed	Some of the timetable is set but all is managed by the student
Teachers know students by name	Students unknown to lecturers
Regular homework set	No fixed pattern
Interact with same group of people every day	Meet new people/groups frequently
Teacher asks for homework/ assignments	Students are seldom, if ever, asked for coursework/ assignments
Students make mistakes and parents write notes	Students make mistakes and work out their own solutions

School	College
Teachers and parents solve problems for or with the student	Students are expected to solve their own problems
Attendance records taken	Attendance records rarely taken
Teachers constantly advise	Students have to seek out advice
System is small and easy to follow	System is large and complicated
Day is tightly structured	Day is generally loosely structured
Dress code applies	Dress code seldom applies
Student usually works alone to achieve academic results	Students work alone and in groups to achieve results
Small classes	Large classes
Discipline is tight	Adult behaviour is expected
Excuses accepted for unfinished homework	Excuses not tolerated for missed deadlines

School	**College**
Dependent learning	Independent learning
Calendar year uniform throughout schools	Calendar year structures different at each college
Teachers recognise changes in behaviours	Changes in behaviour go unnoticed and are difficult to identify
Students are carried by teachers to reach pre-set goals	Sole responsibility falls on student to reach own self-determined goals
Progress is monitored by teachers so problems can be identified early	Progress is monitored by student so problems escalate quickly
Students are informed about rules and regulations by teachers and school principal	Students must become informed by reading all rules and regulations in the college and course handbooks

I have chosen to discuss these differences in broad categories as follows:

> Fitting in socially
> Change in communication channels
> Changing relationships
> Independent learning
> Changing finances

The academic issues and challenges will also be discussed in detail in chapter 4, Day to day life at college.

Fitting in socially

› Have you ever walked alone into a crowded room without knowing anyone?
› Have you ever had that feeling that everyone knows everyone else except you?

You're not sure of what you should say or do, where to sit or who to approach first? Everyone seems tied up in conversation and you may feel uncomfortable about making an effort to join in.

To make matters slightly worse, you may have thought that you were suitably dressed on leaving your home that morning but suddenly you feel that your choice of wearing a multi-coloured bright shirt just may have been the wrong choice of clothing for this occasion.

You force yourself, under pressure, to make random introductions to people but deep down all you want to do is to flee right back into the comfort zone of old familiar surroundings. You may even question why you were there at all.

Transfer these feelings to the first orientation session or lecture you attend at college and then we can perhaps identify some of the first major challenges you encounter at college:

› Meeting new faces in new places
› Going from the familiar to the unfamiliar
› Moving out of your comfort zone
› Leaving the sense of belonging behind you
› Moving away from a community of students which you have interacted with for many years

Conversely, the opposite dilemma can arise. You might feel that you are getting stuck with one set of pals, all from your old school or community, who plan to/are attending the same college. Peer pressure demands that you all remain limited to the same group. You just can't work up the courage to branch out and be free to meet new people and friends without feeling scrutiny from others.

For many this first encounter can also be a very exciting and totally positive experience. You might be looking forward to the next stage of your education for a variety of reasons which include:

› Becoming more independent
› Having freedom
› Doing what you want to do
› Meeting new people
› Studying abroad
› Taking responsibility for yourself
› Studying courses and subjects of interest to you
› Getting a new start
› Socialising

You might also be a little worried by these first steps into the unknown. The pressures of making new friends, of being loyal to old ones, of not looking foolish, can bring on anxieties and fears. These fears niggle in the background and can include:

> I'm afraid I won't fit in and make new friends
> Coming from a single sex school, I don't know how I will handle the gender mix in college
> I'm afraid I will make the same mistakes I made in secondary school
> I want to make new friends but the group I hang around with are all going to the same college and I hate the idea of more of the same
> I'm worried about moving away from home
> I hope that I will like college
> I'm worried I won't be able to achieve academically
> I feel under pressure to perform

These are perfectly normal feelings and for most will pass without too much complication. Many students cope extremely well with this transition and welcome the fresh start in life. Others struggle and can become overpowered with these concerns and by the many academic challenges of college life which are addressed in greater detail in chapter 4, Day to day life at College.

Friends are important. The want to belong to a community of people is great within all of us. At college, you will meet lots of new people and make lasting friendships. These friendships will shape and define your student life, make the experience worthwhile, be a source of fun and relief, provide a crutch in difficult times and act as a gauge on your own progress.

Spare a thought for your parents. Probably, for the first time in almost 18 years, they will not know anything about your new friends and acquaintances or their activities. They may never meet these people or indeed their families, a practice somewhat alien to the comfortable set up of second level school where there are endless opportunities to meet your friends at family or community events and/or sporting and school events.

This comfort scaffolding of the second level order, discipline and familiarity is no longer available at college and you, the student, have to take control and responsibility and make all the decisions about your social development in quite a short period of time.

By the very nature of course delivery, you will be required to interact on a daily basis at lectures and other academic activities in college. You may work alone and in groups but you will need the support of fellow students to stay the course hence the need to build a network quickly. Building a network requires interaction which extends far beyond the lecture theatres.

College life offers more than an academic experience. It allows you to expand and develop socially in an environment which encourages freedom of expression and movement. This social development is key to establishing networks, learning to know the new systems and how they work giving opportunity to try new things at different points during college life, to explore without commitment, offering experiences not to be missed.

Opportunities to network can be lost if you spend hours commuting to college and are unable for this reason to participate in events outside of the set timetables during the day. Economic pressures may also force you to limit time in college to solely addressing the academic requirements.

While it is ultimately your responsibility to successfully manage this development, your parents can assist by chatting informally about these issues if and when possible. As you face into your last cycle of study at second level, you are moving to the senior positions in your school, becoming king/queen of the walk not realising that within a short period, you will start at the bottom rung of the ladder once again. The difference this time is that you are in the driving seat as you independently launch yourself into the college experience.

College clubs and societies are an integral part of the solution regarding adapting to the new social scene in college. Following a sporting interest from the side-line can be as much fun as being part of the team. Societies engage in furthering the academic and social interests of their members. Many of these societies engage in charity work and fundraising activities. You can retain your current interests within these clubs or societies but more importantly you can develop new ones.

While your main goal should be to complete an academic course of study, your social interaction and development is an equally important and integral part of the college experience.

Change in communication channels

At school the relationship is between the school, your parent and you. At college, the relationship is between you and college. This can be very difficult for your parents. Unlike school, college will not write to them, phone them or initiate any contact with them concerning your progress or lack of progress. Neither will their enquiries regarding such progression be warmly received.

School	College

The college learning contract is with you, the student. Your parents will be totally reliant on a healthy and open relationship with you to find out any information regarding your engagement with college.

While all colleges respect the fact that your parents may wish to discuss your progress for a variety of reasons, the colleges are not authorised to disclose such information other than in most exceptional circumstances which is a matter for each individual college authority. If you consent to such communication or request that your parents are consulted regarding any issues, then the college will be happy to comply.

Most of the communication from the college is routine and concerns administrative issues such as: registration, fees, timetabling, college notices, examination details and results. This communication can be made using the following and more:

> Traditional post and noticeboards
> Websites
> Email
> E-noticeboard
> Handbooks
> Content management systems
> Online learning environments
> Social media sites

Colleges are increasingly using the online medium thus reducing or eliminating the need for the more traditional postal and noticeboard type of communication.

Each college and course will have its own unique way of communicating with you. In the spirit of academic freedom, each college lecturer will also have his/her own unique way of communicating with you. It is up to you to learn how the system works with your college and with each of the individual lecturers and/or course directors, where and if applicable.

Students can be absent-minded and not give adequate consideration to the fact that deadlines *mean* deadlines at college. You are coming from a second level system where reminders are issued frequently, where your parents are involved in all these processes and the problems of overdue assignments/payments/registrations are always easily resolved with a handwritten note. Such practices are not tolerated at college.

Third level colleges cater for thousands of students. If each student attending decided to ignore deadlines, be they academic or administrative, the result would be utter chaos. Hence, colleges are unforgiving regarding imposing penalties. We all know that in the real world deadlines have to be met, the show must go on and excuses are not entertained. Being careless about meeting deadlines at college costs money, time or marks. It may cost all three. The rules regarding deadlines are clearly set out in the course and/or college handbook/s.

Whether living at home or away from home, the same problems present. There are advantages and disadvantages to both. See chapter 8, Living at home or away.

Once you gain a greater understanding of day to day life at college which is detailed in chapter 4, it will become evident how further cracks in the communication channels could begin to appear.

Changing relationships
Over the last number of decades, parents have generally made more deliberate efforts to engage their children in set activities and projects, all with the aim of academic betterment. This is reflected by the rising participation rates at third level. You may have become quite dependent on this generation of parents who, up to now, may have organised and imposed such activities at every possible opportunity for a variety of reasons, be it for occupation or entertainment.

On completing second level, the goalposts move and you are expected to adapt quickly to a system of managing your own time, taking control and responsibility for yourself and the organisation of all your activities. The time has come for you to break free as you seek out a new life of your own, one to make your own decisions, to disengage from the conventions and constraints of the second level system and work towards becoming independent of parents and family members. The biggest challenge of all for parents at this time is to listen and to support without interfering.

You are coming from a system where you are chased if you wear the wrong shoes, are late for class or run in the corridor, or don't complete homework. Equally you are praised for academic or sporting achievements and/or the many contributions to active citizenship within your community or school. Whether the experience is positive or negative, you may not know it or even admit that you could miss the caring, the nurturing, the handholding and the familiarity of these exchanges throughout the school day. Love it or hate it, it has been an integral part of your life. As you move out of this supported structure, your parent remains the only constant in your life. This relationship is entering a time of great change, a time when communication can and may break down for a variety of reasons. Much of the solution lies in getting the balance right.

The relationship between you and college is transient. It will last for as long as you attend the institution. Your relationship with your parent/s is forever - be it good, bad or indifferent.

While your parents have no obvious rights to information about your engagement with college they can:

› Listen
› Tune in
› Become informed
› Express interest
› Praise, encourage, motivate and support
› Understand what is normal for you

Independent learning

You come from a largely prescriptive second level system where reward is generally given for the regurgitation of facts and the reliance has been historically on memorisation and rote learning. Attendance throughout the school day is compulsory and tightly monitored with teachers regularly reminding you about homework assignments and your parents writing explanatory notes to the school. This will not happen in college. Everything moves at a faster pace. You are exposed to greater course content over shorter periods of time. It is not unusual for you to feel somewhat at sea at your first few lectures.

Problems can first arise where you find yourself in a troubled state about getting to grips with a particular subject and you may choose to miss a lecture or two which only makes matters worse. Within a short number of weeks the teaching term is well under way and then you may enter a state of panic in the lead up to examinations.

Problems of this nature escalate quickly at third level. Unlike the second level system, the fact that you have fallen behind goes unnoticed at college. You will rarely, if ever, get a chance to fully catch up on lectures you may have missed. The secret here is to identify any academic difficulties at the earliest possible stages and work towards finding a solution, a solution which might rest with fellow students or with lecturers or with the student supports offered within the colleges services. This is explained further in chapter 7, Making use of the services.

You and your parent/s might question why the awarding of high grades in the second level system does not automatically transfer to the college system. At college examiners seek, as a minimum, a demonstration of a good understanding of the subject under study and reward the ability to critically analyse and interpret relevant theories leading to their application in a practical professional way.

Learning to learn is a skill for life. Doing well in college is about acquiring the art of independent learning, becoming an active learner and taking control of the individual learning process. Some students naturally embrace this challenge while others take some time to acquire the skill.

Taking ownership and responsibility for your learning is probably the greatest challenge of all at college. This is further addressed in chapter 9, Becoming a successful student.

Changing finances

Finance now plays a bigger role than ever in the journey through college as families struggle to work, to pay the mortgage, put food on the table and to maintain some semblance of normal family life. High taxes, lower wages and salaries and a somewhat unstable economy make the financial future more uncertain for all. Everyone reading this book has been affected by the economic downturn. The fallout and subsequent decisions arising are different across families. No matter what circumstances prevail, no matter what dreams and aspirations you may have, the facts are that there is a rising price tag on third level education today and someone has to pay the bill.

For the most part, the family bears the financial responsibility of bringing the student through the second level system but as the student progresses to the next level, things change. In some cases, the family continues to bear this financial responsibility, however, for many this is not the case as more students now depend on grant aid, part-time work, scholarships and in some cases the support of extended family to bring them through their years of study.

While living away from home brings an enormous additional financial pressure on families, there is also great cost for those students living at home. Regardless of where you live, it is a very big cost. Many students make significant contributions to their upkeep. Contribution to assist the family can take many forms and may not always be financial. It may take the form of caring for junior family members, elderly or dependent relatives or simply by playing a meaningful role in the domestic running of the household.

› Have you thought about how you could make your contribution?

A balanced approach to taking up part-time work in college is necessary. When making this decision, due consideration must be given to assessing the academic workload associated with the particular course of study. For some, part-time work may not fit in with a demanding college schedule and may negatively impact on academic performance. On the other hand, it may be perfectly feasible to work for a few hours each week without a conflict of interest. Most students look for work during summer breaks, some at home and many abroad. Such work develops a sense of responsibility and accountability, generates entrepreneurship and makes a good impression on any prospective employer.

The discussion of who pays the bills is extremely important and should be addressed before you start college. This should deal broadly with the full college commitment but in the first instance with how the first year is handled. Over the course of the first year there will be lots of discussion with fellow students as to how the first or second summer college holidays might be spent. Many students become determined to spend this time abroad. The most obvious questions here are:

› Where does the money come from to fund the cost of flights and accommodation and any necessary insurance?
› Is there work available and how will you find it?

Travelling abroad is exciting but often difficult situations can arise particularly if friends become separated or some of the travelling party change travel plans for a variety of reasons at the last minute.

If you are planning to work outside the country for the summer months during college, it is highly recommended that health insurance cover is purchased *before* leaving the country. Special packages are widely available for students for this purpose.

In particular this is most important when travelling outside the EU. Many students travelling to the United States, Canada and further afield are unaware of the implications of travelling without adequate health insurance. It is also important to establish if there are any special travel visas or vaccinations required within your travel zone. If travelling within the EU, you should seek to obtain a European Health Insurance Card (EHIC) which carries certain health entitlements within the EU.

You will need to contact Citizens Information to establish the eligibility rules for the EHIC card and to find out any other information regarding overseas travel in general. See the useful links section at the end of the book.

This chapter has identified many differences between the two systems. Some students will struggle more than others in embracing the changes. Your social and academic development is dependent on how you become informed, take ownership and responsibility and face up to the many challenges presenting.

The next chapter, Day to day life at college, will seek to bring some clarity about what happens at college and help you to understand and deal with these challenges.

Chapter 4

DAY TO DAY LIFE AT COLLEGE

Having already addressed the importance of choosing the right study path and the main differences between the second level and third level systems, this chapter looks at how the college system is structured and the business it engages in from day to day, the business with which you will be concerned with for three to four years.

Before considering the day to day life at college, it is important to understand a little about how the academic year is structured.

Academic year structure

Semesters
Semesters comprise two long terms over the academic year which can run for 12 to 15 weeks and which may include an examination period – this depends on whether the course is modularised.

Modularisation
If a college uses a modularised system it generally means that at the end of each semester there is a formal examination period. If the course is not fully modularised then the formal examinations from both semester 1 and 2 may be held at the end of the academic year.

This might be something you need to consider when choosing particular courses and colleges.

Terms
Some colleges continue to refer to and work in traditional terms of three, one before Christmas, one immediately after Christmas and one Spring/Summer. These terms can vary in length but usually comprise a set number of weeks each. The following is a typical example of how these three terms could be broken up over the academic year:

> Term 1:   8 to 10 weeks
> Term 2:   8 to 10 weeks
> Term 3   6 to 8 weeks

In this case, it is more usual to sit one set of formal examinations at the end of the academic year.

The academic year structure will vary from college to college, faculty to faculty, department to department, and course to course. Some colleges/courses adopt a mixture of all of the above. You will be guided through this process in the handbook/s relating to your particular course.

What is most important for you to find out early on in college:

> What deadlines have to be met in the first semester/term
> When the first assignments are due
> When the first formal examinations take place
> The implications of these deadlines, assignments and examinations for your end of year results

The major differences between the second level and third level systems have been detailed in chapter 3. Getting to understand these differences can be a slow process. However, as you begin to accept just how different these two systems are, you come to appreciate the importance of mastering your own timetable and seeking to generate opportunities to progress your academic and social development.

The academic demands imposed on you at college revolve around three fundamentals within any course of study:

> Learning objectives and outcomes
> Methods of teaching and delivery
> Assessment

The learning outcomes are determined by the lecturing staff in conjunction with course directors and course committees all of which can be at faculty level or department/school level within the faculty, depending on the institution concerned.

Methods of teaching and delivery will vary from college to college and course to course and will generally be outlined in the handbooks for all courses. This will be discussed in more detail in the section 'Interactions at College' in this chapter.

Methods of assessment also vary from college to college and course to course. In all cases you will sit a number of formal examinations either at the end of semesters/terms or at the end of the academic year or both. You will also be examined over the course of the year and can be assessed using various methods of continuous assessment from coursework assignments to practical demonstrations and presentations. This will be dealt with further in this chapter and in chapter 6, The college examination process.

No two colleges or courses are identical in their learning outcomes, modes of delivery or the associated assessment process. Many factors influence this including the academic freedom afforded to the lecturing community, the huge variation in college and class sizes and the multiple methods of delivery and assessment of the curricula. No one size fits all. Hence it is important that the choice of college is factored into choosing the right course which has already been discussed in chapter 2, Choosing your study path.

Over your time in college, you will engage in the many interactions listed. While this list is not exhaustive it is illustrative of the general type of activities encountered. These vary in terminology and in application from college to college and from course to course.

Sometimes parents may base the college experience entirely on lecture hours, more often referred to as 'contact' hours and can be unaware of the many other day to day activities that can take place and how these activities impact on your overall experience. The lecture hours are only one part of this experience.

Interactions at College
> Registration
> Orientation
> Choosing Electives
> Lectures
> Library
> Electronic learning systems and supports
> Tutorials/Seminars
> Laboratories/Demonstrations/Practicals
> Research
> Coursework/Assignments/Portfolios
> Examinations
> Study
> Revision/Study/Reading weeks
> Group work
> Independent learning
> Academic writing
> Academic offences
> Freshers' week
> Societies
> Sports clubs
> Students' Union

Registration
When you attend college, you are required to formally register as a student and pay the relevant fee. In fact, all students attending third level must register every year as a matter of course. Little further explanation is required. Most colleges are now operating this system online. A date for registration will be sent to you. It is most important that you register at the appointed time as fines will be imposed for late registrations. Generally, following registration, student identity cards are issued.

It is also important to note that you cannot sit the official college examinations if you are not formally registered as a student at the college. You may also be denied access to electronic systems and supports.

Orientation
Each college will have its own unique way of introducing you to the campus and its facilities, with colleges setting aside a number of days/weeks for this process. This introduction referred to as 'Orientation' provides you with an opportunity to familiarise yourself with the campus and can include:

›   The location of the buildings you will frequent
›   The library
›   The type of operations/systems the college employs
›   Communication methods
›   The range of facilities provided
›   Modes of delivery of syllabus
›   Support services
›   College rules and traditions
›   Key events
›   Key academic dates
›   and much more

Local induction sessions are also held for students and can be held during or outside the formal college orientation period. These sessions are more course specific and attendance is essential if you are serious about your commitment to study.

It is most important that you attend all orientation/induction sessions as it is here that myths are dispelled and fears are allayed and the beginning of long friendships are formed. Too often, some students and indeed parents alike see these sessions as unimportant. When difficulties arise, be they of an academic or social nature, the old familiar sounds of "that was covered at Orientation" tends to haunt these students who feel that they have missed out on key information during those few days.

This feeling is comparable to arriving half-way through the movie and while the plot unfolds you constantly find yourself asking questions about who fits in where, much to the displeasure of the surrounding audience. Add the complication of examination regulations to the college scenario and the pressure begins to grow rapidly.

Choosing Electives

Usually on each course you will take core modules/subjects which are compulsory and other option modules. You can also choose Elective modules which allow you to deepen your knowledge of the core or option modules or to explore subjects unrelated to your main subject area.

All modules/subjects studied at college are allocated a number of credits under the European Credit Transfer and Accumulation System (ECTS), a standardised system within Europe which measures student performance at third level and facilitates national and international mobility within the academic system.

The important thing for you to look out for when choosing modules is if this choice will negatively impact the choices available to you in the subsequent years of your course at your college or at a college abroad. It would also be useful to check how these modules are assessed.

Lectures

This is the traditional tuition normally delivered by academics. You are given a broad account of the course or subject under study. This process can take many forms from the more traditional instruction to the interactive/practical, to the more recent introduction of virtual learning environments. The lecturer may seek interaction, however, in the larger lecture theatres which can accommodate hundreds of students, this becomes less likely.

The focus of the lecture is to give you the fundamentals and the core teaching relating to a subject. You are then expected to research the topic under study and build on the fundamentals into a more detailed study, all in your own time. This is the first point where you may feel uncomfortable in how to approach this task and the seeds of self-direction in the learning process are set.

Attendance at lectures is a basic college requirement and you should make every effort to be on time. It is good practice and good manners. While this attendance is generally voluntary and entirely within your control, some colleges may impose the rule of compulsory attendance. Occasionally 'in class' exercises may be conducted and collected, an attendance list by another means. Failure to attend such lectures may risk poor performance or even failure. See chapters on the college examination process and handbooks.

Academic concepts and theories are introduced and explored at lectures but once dealt with, are seldom repeated. Hence the need to attend all lectures, develop good note taking skills and to develop good listening skills. Administrative matters raised by lecturers will generally be raised once and once only. A typical example of this might be a deadline announced for the submission of assignment work.

You will need to get to know the individual style of each lecturer and this will become apparent quite early on. It is important to understand that the lecturer is concerned with his or her subject only and it is in this context that you slowly realise that your timetable needs to be managed carefully, juggling the demands placed by the various lecturers within the many subjects studied on any course.

Remember the lecturer is also the examiner. Given this situation, obvious signs may be often given such as "note this carefully" or "this is probably the most important part of" or "students always forget that" or "what I find on examination papers is that students fail to recognise..."

At first, you will find it hard to understand what information is important and what is not. This is perfectly normal and this skill will develop as you progress through the first year exploring further subjects and engaging in academic debate on the many opinions on these subjects. The lecture is only one of the many activities at the heart of your working week.

Library
The library is the cornerstone of all learning and an essential and integral resource for all students attending third level. The library can take two forms; that of the physical building or electronic form or a combination of both. Its value can't be overstressed. You will be introduced to the library and the associated processes during Orientation and you should avail of this opportunity. It is so important for you to become familiar with both the traditional and the electronic library systems as early as possible during your time in college.

You can feel intimidated on the first visits to the library regardless of location of the facility, on or offline. You will find it difficult to know where to look for material, unable at first to discern the relevant from the irrelevant or the good from the mediocre.

Lecturers and demonstrators will guide you through this process by gradually introducing you to the key authors in the field which you are studying. As you gain confidence in the subject area and become familiar with the key concepts and theories addressed by these authors, you will then begin to explore ideas further by reading and researching around the subject. This will happen over time as you incrementally acquire the skill of making good judgement regarding that which is relevant and of academic credibility.

The art of referencing academic work goes hand in hand with the library and with all writing in the course of your study. It is most important that you understand the implications of correctly referencing academic work early on in your academic experience. This can prove a daunting experience for some. However, this should not be the case as the library/college support systems provide regular support for all in learning this art.

An investment in time in becoming competent in using library facilities, college online facilities and academic referencing can repay the effort involved in terms of learning, achievement and even level of degree finally reached.

All courses will have reading lists, comprising some core essential reference books and some recommended reading. The library holds a limited stock of all books whether essential or recommended reading. Students who are there early get the best picking either within the library building or in many cases to take out on loan for a number of weeks. Some students buy a limited set of core text books which may be required over a number of years of the course of study. Others join together and share the cost, however, the distribution and collection of these books in a shared system can be problematic.

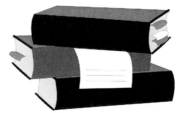

Libraries impose fines on students for books which are overdue. In most colleges, students must pay outstanding fines before being allowed to graduate with their year.

Electronic learning systems and supports
Each college will have its own electronic systems which, in the first instance, cater for the administrative functions within the college. These will typically include:

> Registration
> Timetabling
> Examination systems
> Grading systems
> Fee payments
> Academic awards

Various content management systems are employed by the colleges to facilitate online access by you to academic material. In some courses, online teaching and tutorials may be adopted which can facilitate students whether on campus, at home or in a workplace.

More and more colleges are using teaching and learning technologies to support the learning experience. Some colleges and courses are more advanced in their use than others and the developments are on-going.

The things for you to note as a first time student are those concerning registration, deadlines, key dates and key notices - both academic and administrative, timetabling and examination structures which can include notification of time, place and in due course, results.

It is quite possible that you can engage in college activity over the course of a given academic year, sit examinations and obtain results without your parent knowing if you have attended college at all or how you have performed at examinations.

In essence, you can do your own thing for a full year at college and your parent/s may be none the wiser one year on. This is not possible at second level.

Tutorials/Seminars
Tutorials take place in small groups and are generally centred around your lectures. These can be facilitated by lecturers, teaching assistants or demonstrators who are appointed by the various course directors and committees. Tutorials offer you an opportunity to discuss issues which arise during the formal lecture but which due to time constraints can't be elaborated on at that time. They afford you opportunities for debate through interactions with academic staff where both work together to find solutions and avenues for further exploration.

Tutorials are an integral part of the learning process and students find them extremely useful in progressing to a deeper level of understanding in their chosen subject areas. Attendance is very often compulsory and students are regularly assessed both by their attendance and by their level of interaction. Students wishing to optimise the experience come prepared and are better placed to contribute positively to discussion. Tutorials can take different formats, for example, Science subjects may have practical elements quite different from the tutorials within the Arts/Humanities subjects.

Seminars can be college, industry or student-led and like tutorials provide an opportunity to deepen the learning experience in a particular subject area. Some may be strictly informative while others take a more problem-solving approach, relying on student participation.

Laboratories /Demonstrations/Practicals

Often referred to as labs or demos, these can vary in format and delivery and can be held in scientific laboratories, computer based laboratories, small meeting rooms, on site or field visits, and at various offsite locations. Generally facilitated by postgraduate demonstrators, these sessions offer students the opportunity to learn by practice, experimentation and problem solving.

You will need to familiarise yourself with the various formats by carefully reading the associated course/college handbook/s. As with the lectures and tutorials, attendance may be compulsory and you should refer to the handbooks to establish if this is the case.

Presentations

Presentations are becoming a more integral part of the academic experience at college. Students are regularly required to make presentations individually or as part of a group. These presentations are almost always assessed as part of the annual examination process. You will need to work hard on making any visual aids used relevant, readable and interesting in the subject area. Visual aids should be uncluttered in presentation. You will need to practice your presentation and consider how you present yourself, how you speak and how you interact with your audience. These are essential transferable skills which are widely sought after in today's workplace.

With presentations you need to:

> Know and understand the brief
> Know the purpose
> Know and understand your audience
> Know your subject
> Be clear about your method of delivery

In case of equipment failure, some kind of contingency plan is essential which could include:

› Notes on one side of a page/card
   - Numbered and in order
› Stored in sequence
   - Which can be easily read

Practice is an integral part of any preparation and good preparation will determine your success.

If you are depending on technology to make presentations and to meet deadlines, disaster can strike. The technology may not be compatible, may be unreliable or simply may not work in spite of test runs. Lecture theatres and meeting rooms are used by hundreds of students and many staff so it is inevitable that on occasions this multiple use will lead to problems.

It is vital that you have your work supported independently in an electronic format as proof of work done by a specified date. Otherwise, you risk gaining no marks for work done and ultimate failure of an examination. Lecturers take a particularly hard line on this issue and rightly so, given the wide range of portable hardware devices and cloud computing solutions available. It is advisable to save your work to at least two locations and in different formats.

Research

Research, like teaching and learning, is the core business of third level institutions. It can be simply defined as finding out important facts and information about a subject. It can be described as discovering new insights, new knowledge or combining existing knowledge, finding out what the key authors on a subject are writing about and how the subject is viewed and interpreted by academia, industry and society. The degree to which research is conducted varies and is usually determined by the academic demands placed on the student at a particular stage in the academic cycle of study.

Research can lead to new and unexpected discovery of theories and applications which contribute to the development and shape of the world we live in from social, cultural and economic perspectives. In the course of researching, the student reads to gather information, to analyse and interpret findings and to adopt an academic style of writing.

Reading is a skill in itself and incorporates the art of scanning, skimming, normal reading and close reading. Understanding is more important than speed. Students tend to learn this process in incremental stages at third level.

In the early stages of research you need to know what is expected of you. Guidance is given at lectures and tutorials. Useful questions include:

› What do I need to know?
› What are the time limits?
› How do I gather information?
› What resources will I need?
› Where can I go to find these resources?
› How can I use Information Technology to best advantage in this process?

Over time you gather the information, then progress to evaluating it and within time begin to become a critical reader and thinker in the context of credibility of sources, academic argument and how this fits within your stage of learning.

In your first year, you may be taught by leading professors and researchers in the field of your chosen study. When you attend tutorials you will also have opportunities to interact with postgraduate students who work at the cutting edge of research within research groups.

All colleges foster research and innovation from within and offer supports to students who bring new ideas to successful business ventures through their research in the course of their college studies. It is not unusual that students set up new businesses while in their first few years at college. Such activity is widely encouraged within the college and student community and workshops are often held to develop ideas.

Coursework/Assignments/Portfolios
These are examinations by another name and can present as essays, project work, multiple choice questions, presentations, portfolios, and other and may be examined as practical or clinical work, by oral demonstrations or as a body of written work. These are opportunities to apply theory, simulate professional practice and to consolidate learning. The terms 'coursework' and 'continuous assessment' are interchangeably used in this context.

This work is allocated a percentage of marks which contributes to the overall examination result within any course of study in the academic year. This is clearly set out in the handbooks for the particular course under study. Penalties are usually imposed for late submissions and in some cases these can be quite severe resulting in failure due to lateness rather than academic ability.

Should the late submission of work be the sole reason for failure, the college will generally treat this as a breach of college rules. In certain circumstances, the student may be afforded an opportunity to resubmit. It can also be the case that a student may have passed the formal examinations at the end of the semesters/academic year but may end up having to change summer plans simply because of a missed 'Coursework' deadline.

It is important to recognise the value of retaining copies of all written coursework whether in paper or electronic form. Backing up files on computers/laptops at regular intervals and on completion/ submission of academic work will save disappointment at some stage of your college journey.

Adopting good habits early on pays dividends. You should also note that marks are, in almost all cases, awarded for the formatting and presentation of coursework. Don't waste them.

Refer to your course handbook/s for rules relating to all of the above.

Examinations
Chapter 6, The college examination process, is dedicated solely to this topic.

Study
As you can see your day is now filling up with lectures, tutorials, group work, demonstrations and other but that 'study' word still has to be addressed. Managing your timetable and fitting in study time can be stressful and challenging. If you have low 'contact/ lecture hours', for example, as Arts or Law students, you will have to be more self-directed in your remaining hours unlike fellow Engineering or Science students who will have higher 'contact/ lecture hours' with a more fixed schedule.

All students, regardless of course of study, need to develop a consistent approach to study given the nature of the demand of assignments and other work set as part of the continuous assessment process.

So just how much study time is required?

It is impossible to accurately gauge what study time is required as this will vary from student to student, from course to course, and from type of subject undertaken within any course of study. This will also depend greatly on how you learn and how you study and the academic demands placed on you.

A good check of how the study is going at any given time during the academic year might be to look at past examination papers relating to the subject area.

Revision/Study/Reading weeks
At many colleges, revision/study/reading weeks may be offered to students during each semester or close to examination time. Usually no formal college lectures take place at this time, however, some colleges may run presentations, orals and practical assessments during these weeks.

The practice varies from college to college and course to course. Some students confuse this with holiday time. If such a week is built into your course, it is assigned specifically to you for the purposes of reading up on course material, working on unfinished assignments and generally catching up on college work and taking time to reflect on your overall performance to date.

It is a good opportunity to revise material covered in any course of study and to identify gaps to assess strengths and weaknesses. It can also be a good time to hone study plans for the remainder of the semester/year and to identify any college services which may help you along the way.

Group work
Students on almost all courses in college will have to collaborate with other students forming groups in which they work together to a common goal, often towards the production of a report or

assignment or the building of a product or the development of a research idea.

You can't be under the illusion that you will attend college for three or four years and work alone. This will never be the case as interaction with others is a necessary part of the academic and social development of every student. Whether working in industry, the professions or business, working as part of a team is vital and employers rate it as a very important skill.

Working in groups can often be quite difficult as many challenges present. On some courses students can self-select while on other courses this selection is imposed by course directors or coordinators. Both ways can prove problematic as groups must develop into teams before they begin to work effectively together.

The discussion regarding the fundamental differences of working in groups and teams is a subject in its own right. Getting the right balance within groups can be equally challenging for both the strong and weak students. The stronger students often feel they have to carry the weaker while the weaker can feel intimated by the stronger. The hard-working student often feels an intolerable burden while the easy-going student can plod along knowing that someone else will pick up the pieces. Sounds like a reflection of real life, real families, and real workplaces and it is.

Working in groups is a process that needs to be managed towards an effective outcome. In order to do this, ground rules must be set and adhered to, just like running a home or fielding a team.

There is sometimes mixed opinion as to the value of teamwork particularly in the case of assessment, however, the ability to work in teams and to become part of a team remains an integral part of the academic activity within any course of study at most colleges.

Employers look for skilled graduates who are problem solvers and are comfortable working with others to achieve results.

Independent learning
The art of independent learning has received a lot of mention so far in this book. Chapter 9, How to become a successful student, focuses on this art.

Academic writing
You may have memories of Shakespeare from school and whether it was the study of King Lear, Macbeth or Romeo and Juliet, many can probably recite passages at will. We could say that Shakespeare went about making his point in a rather complex manner, using heightened language which required significant work in its interpretation. So to some extent, you entered into the spirit of the time, parsing and analysing passages for deeper meaning and finding ways of applying this to ordinary daily living either in its time or analysing its relevance to our own time.

If we transfer this concept to any study at third level, for example, Science, Language, Business, Law, Education or Health, each subject has its own particular language, its own set of words associated with that subject and/or profession. Like studying Shakespeare, you too must familiarise yourself with the language of your subject and take the time to learn to appreciate, understand and develop the particular language and how it is expressed within your course of study.

Academic writing has its own unique style and each subject/ discipline has its own unique terminology. Some students adapt quickly to this style and terminology but most take some time to learn it.

Through the college library system you can learn this art by reading:

> Text books
> Academic papers
> Technical papers
> Conference proceedings
> The academic work of other students

A different style of writing is also required for different demands such as:

> Essay writing
> Report writing
> Project work
> Management reports

Colleges offer supports to students to assist in developing these different writing styles.

Academic offences

One of the greatest academic offences is that of plagiarism where the student takes the work of others and calls it his or her own.

Plagiarism is serious. It can mean failure or expulsion. In academic writing or presentation, all authors' work must be acknowledged. Cutting and pasting from the web is not tolerated. Lecturers and examiners can tell very quickly when a student is committing this offence as they are expert in the field of their own studies. Electronic tools are also used by lecturers to examine students' work for plagiarism as it is submitted for assessment. Students who commit this offence may be precluded from sitting examinations.

Other offences can include:

›   Carrying and use of mobile technology during examinations
›   Unacceptable use of social media and technology while conducting academic and college business

A lot of this is common sense. However, if and when sanctions are imposed for such offences, the rules applying within the college and course handbooks will ultimately apply.

Freshers' week

No book dealing with the subject of transition to third level could be complete without due mention of Freshers' week. Freshers' week often coincides with Orientation but they are not one and the same thing.

Fresher's week is an exciting and eventful week during which you are introduced to college life, to sports, clubs and societies, and are persuaded, cajoled and often bribed by a mere pizza slice to sign up.

During this week many extra events are put on to get you out and about and socialising with others. The fun is infectious across campus and the fever spreads to the more senior student community who often oversee the organisation and planning of these events in conjunction with the Students' Union office.

Freshers' week is usually the first encounter that your parents have with you being out all day and late at night, often every night, offering little or no explanation as to your whereabouts. At this time, the lines of communication can become a little more complicated than desired. Tempers can be challenged. If you are living away from home, your parents may be oblivious to such activity which is all the more reason why you might like to read chapter 8, Living at home or away.

Freshers' week can be such a fun time, a time where new chapters begin, a time to get involved.

Societies

Societies are an integral part of college life, are run by students, and receive support from the Students' Union within college. Societies differ in their goals but in the main are run to promote hobbies or special interests, to engage in professional development and to organise volunteering and fundraising activities for various charities. They facilitate interaction between like-minded students with many interests which can include the following and many more:

> Business
> Politics
> Foreign languages
> History
> Law
> Computing

> Zoology
> Sign language
> Philosophy
> Knitting
> Geology
> Film
> Music
> Aeronautics
> Engineering
> Chess
> Botany
> Rowing
> Hiking
> Fishing

Competition between societies within colleges and across colleges is strong as students compete annually to have the biggest and the best society seeking to win the many associated prestigious awards. Each year new societies are formed with many budding entrepreneurs emerging. People and project management skills are well tested in such endeavours, skills highly regarded by employers.

Check out what societies are running at your college of choice.

Sports clubs
Sport is at the heart of social activity within colleges and new students are encouraged to join sports clubs during Freshers' week. Students gain endless enjoyment and satisfaction from participation at this level and travel locally, nationally and internationally to represent their colleges at various events. Competition between the colleges is serious.

All teams need fan clubs, so lovers of sport can offer support on the side-line and also play their part by running events and in raising awareness among the wider student communities both within the college or among prospective students.

Students' Union

The Students' Union office is the hub of activity for students in all colleges. Notices of all social activities are found here. Colleges support students in the organisation of many events for the betterment of students and college life. They appoint communication/entertainment officers solely for this purpose. The Students' Union is run by students for students. However, all activities must be run within the set guidelines of college policy relating to such activities.

This office works closely with the Class Reps (see chapter 7) within the colleges and meets regularly to work on new ideas for social development. Together with the Class Reps they can also put forward suggestions for reforms to the college systems to the various college officers and committees.

If you want the most up-to-date information regarding events, best prices, discounts, special deals for students and the latest developments with social media, then the Students' Union is the place to find out what you need to know.

DISCIPLINE

The matter of discipline at college is self-imposed. There is usually no dress code. Students are expected to behave as adults and lecturers will not waste time dealing with disruptive students. It is in your own interest to be attentive and respectful at lectures as every last minute is required to deliver course content. Fellow students will not take kindly to precious time being wasted.

Time lost for unruly behaviour will not be made up and while at times students may feel that college staff are indifferent to their needs, this is where there is an expectation by college that students approach their work from an independent learning perspective.

The inappropriate use of technological equipment on campus is not tolerated. This can include the sharing of passwords and any activity which could threaten security systems or constitute illegal activity or conflict with college rules. Breaches of discipline will be dealt with by disciplinary committees as set out under college rules.

GETTING TO KNOW THE SYSTEM

From all of the above, it can be established that quite a lot of activity takes place in the daily course of business in college. A lot of demands are placed on you as you enter this new system. Getting to know what it is about and how it works is half the battle. This, together with timely application to the academic demands will contribute greatly to making a smooth transition from second level.

The next chapter will address the Handbook.

Chapter 5

HANDBOOKS

This is the shortest but probably the most important chapter in the book.

In every college, every course/subject has some form of a handbook which is presented either in electronic or manual format (or both) and in which there is great detail provided on the rules and regulations and general information surrounding the particular course of study undertaken.

When it comes to rules and regulations and to old fashioned academia, college is king with rules. This is such an important fact for you to know. You must familiarise yourself as soon as possible with the contents of all handbooks introduced on your course. The handbook/s will also need to be revisited at regular intervals throughout the semester/year as different academic demands arise.

If you are studying subjects across more than one department in college, for example, a Business department and a Language department, then two sets of rules apply; one for the Business department and one for the Language department. The presentation of the handbooks will vary from department to department and from college to college. Should your course of study stretch across three different departments within college then a further set of rules may apply.

Added to this, there may be a 'College' rule book/handbook, called by different names in different colleges which you must study in the context of its relevance to your course of study. You must also study this rule book/handbook in the context of being registered as a student of the college as well as on an individual course. The 'College' rule book/handbook is particularly important when dealing with matters such as discipline, examination structures and rules, academic awards, requests relating to withdrawal from courses and long absences such as those relating to health issues or other factors.

You need to read the rules carefully, as quickly as possible, at the beginning of each semester/term and read them on a regular basis throughout the academic year as new experiences relating to the design, delivery and assessment of courses are encountered. Handbooks are updated annually for all courses.

Pleading ignorance of the contents of handbooks falls on deaf ears. It is your responsibility to obtain copies of all relevant handbooks and familiarise yourself with the regulations relating to your course of study. Examples of these are widely available on various college websites.

Typically course handbooks may cover the following and more:

> Course requirements
> Subject/module choices
> Course content
> Learning outcomes
> Methods of delivery
> Assessment
> Referencing styles
> Deadlines
> Timetables
> Key dates
> Location of administrative offices and addressing of related issues
> History of the particular department/s
> Staff details and contact times
> Marking criteria
> Examination structures
> Examination rules and regulations
> Coursework/assignment rules
> Medical certification matters
> Details of tutoring/mentoring/advisory system for students

It is most important to remember that while you might look for clarification in a handbook relating to one department on some aspect of a subject/module under study, you must also check to establish if the same rule applies within the greater 'College' handbook. Should different rules apply, you will need to seek advice from an academic member of staff/course coordinator/course director/tutor or student advisor to establish the correct path to follow.

Should there be conflict of opinion on any matters of this nature, you should, at the earliest possible time, seek clarification in writing of the final decision reached and retain a copy of this for your future reference.

No further elaboration is required on the handbooks except:

READ THE HANDBOOK!!

In chapter 6, we will look at the college examination process.

Chapter 6

THE COLLEGE EXAMINATION PROCESS

The examination process at college is very different to that of the Leaving Certificate system.

Examinations take many formats throughout the year and at the end of the year. Students are examined over the course of the academic year through continuous assessment which may take the title of coursework and present in many forms such as:

> Essays
> Presentations
> Demonstrations
> Orals (can also be referred to as Vivas)
> Participation at tutorials
> Multiple choice questions
> Reports
> Project work
> Analysing problem scenarios
> Analysing case studies
> Portfolios
> Attendance and performance at practicals

A certain percentage of the overall academic grading for the year is allocated to this type of work and as deadlines are met and passed this work is corrected and the results are recorded. The marks achieved through this form of assessment are then filed into the individual student record and at the end of the academic year are added to all other examination results with a final grading being awarded to the student at this time.

Should the student fail any aspect of this coursework, a second opportunity may be offered to the student to resubmit. However, this is highly dependent on the nature of the subject under study, the reasons for the failure and the local rules outlined in the handbook/s and any college rules relating to the particular continuous type of assessment in question.

In all examinations, be they in the form of coursework or formal written examinations, you will be required to present either your student identity card (at written examinations) or a student number (when submitting coursework) to show that you are a registered student of the college. Failure to produce such identification may result in refusal of permission to sit examinations, lost assignments, heartache and an overall very negative experience. You should also note that unless you are formally registered as a student of the college you are not permitted to partake in the formal examination process.

At college, if the academic year structure is fully modularised, then the first formal sitting of examinations takes place at the end of the first semester under strict examination rules and conditions. Local college and course rules will define these. The results of these examinations are also filed and parked after the first semester. A final set of examinations takes place at the end of the academic year/second semester and these marks are then added to the remaining 'parked' results with a final mark awarded. This final mark determines your academic progression within your course of study.

Unlike the second level system, in almost all circumstances, a student who fails a first sitting of a formal written examination is afforded a second opportunity to sit a repeat examination. As the student progresses through to the final years in study, different rules may apply. Local college rules contained in handbooks will determine such opportunities.

It is important to note that if you have long absences from college due to health/other matters which negatively affect your ability to engage in normal academic activities and to sit examinations, college may offer you a separate sitting of these examinations. These sittings will usually be deemed to be first sittings.

All such cases of prolonged absences must be alerted to the course director and/or relevant college authorities *at the time of the absence and in writing*, and be fully supported by evidence from a registered medical practitioner. The governing rules are explained in the college/course handbooks.

With the rules understood, it is equally important to understand why examinations are held at college in the first instance.

What is the purpose of examinations?
Examinations serve many functions including:

> Measuring what learning has taken place over a set period of time and within set material covered
> Providing feedback to students and staff
> Maintaining and developing academic standards
> Ensuring quality control both within the colleges and externally through accreditation by professional bodies

Examinations are designed to assess levels of understanding at a given time and what the student has learned given exposure to a set amount of material within a specific timeframe.

At third level the examiner is looking for a good understanding of the subject matter taught, rewarding evidence of deep engagement where there is the development of sound argument, critical thinking and evaluation. Marking criteria are set out clearly within most subjects/modules under instruction. It is important that you become familiar with these criteria as early as possible and as the material is being delivered in the course of a given semester/term.

It is also important that you become familiar with the various examination terms that can form part of the many active instructions contained in any questions or parts of questions in a given examination paper. These can include:

> Analyse
> Appraise
> Critically appraise
> Argue
> Describe
> Describe briefly
> Develop
> Discuss
> Evaluate
> Critically evaluate
> Examine
> Explain
> Give the main reasons
> Outline
> List
> Review
> State
> Recommend
> Summarise

Of the many terms used, you must work towards a clear understanding of what these terms mean and respond appropriately to the instruction given. Getting used to examination terms and interpreting the correct meaning of these terms is key to doing well at examinations. Samples of previous examination questions will be available to all students who seek them out. Tutorials may provide an ideal opportunity to explore these terms and discuss how you might approach a typical examination question on the topic under discussion.

If you get nervous about examinations, this means you care. Anxiety creeps in around examinations but why do we worry so much about them?

Anxiety affects how we think and behave and is demonstrated by feelings of panic, leaving us in situations where we can't think straight and make sound decisions. If you are too anxious, you may overlook obvious things at examinations such as:

> The question is set in two parts with an either/or option presented
> There is an instruction to answer two out of three questions
> You miss the word 'compulsory'
> You forget to check for questions on both sides of the examination paper

When this happens, handwriting also suffers and often becomes illegible making the examiner's job more difficult.

Fears of examinations arise for many reasons:

> Fear of failure
> Not feeling confident about your subject
> They stir up memories of past examinations
> Negative school experiences
> The importance of this examination in your life
> The fact that everyone knows you are sitting it

A certain amount of nervousness is a good thing. Actors will admit that nervousness creates an adrenaline rush which leads to better performance. If you feel that you are overly nervous, you need to take some steps to help the situation. There are services available in college to help you, see chapter 7. Rest, relaxation and a good diet are very important. Practice deep breathing to keep calm.

You could try to generate similar study conditions to those in a formal examination setting. If you become accustomed to studying with the coffee cup at your side and music playing, it may be difficult to recall information under pressure in the formal examination setting which will be very different from your normal study environment.

Why do students fail examinations?

Simply put, success in examination lies with preparation. The work has to be done. No preparation means failure and poor preparation risks failure. Attendance at lectures, tutorials, demonstrations, laboratory sessions and other is essential. Well documented lecture notes and study notes are invaluable resources in this preparation. Regular self-checks on knowledge of material covered to date will uncover areas which need most attention in your study.

We all use excuses about performance at examinations:

> Not enough time to prepare
> Lecture material wasn't fully covered
> Lecturers were poor
> Useless notes
> Too much work
> Too many pressures
> Too many conflicting deadlines
> The system is unfair

Whatever the excuses, your peers are in the same situation and are being tested on the same material. This is a time for you to take control.

Start as you intend to continue. This sounds like common sense and it is. Develop your research and study skills early on. Each time you set about doing research/study always set yourself a question.

Ask yourself:

› What am I trying to achieve in this session?
› What question am I answering?

Get to know your own strengths and weaknesses and learn to work around them. How does your memory work? Develop methods which suit you best, these could include:

› Lists
› Acronyms
› Association of names and places
› Rhyme
› Song (practice this one in your head)

A good idea would be to think how you might structure your answers - maybe with a simple beginning, middle and an end, just like presentations. Different subjects and questions require different approaches.

Practice several ways of handwriting at speed about the subject, in lengthy theoretical explanations and in shorter, main points, expressed as bullet points. This is important particularly if on the one hand long essay style answers are expected and equally important if you are required to pull out the bullet points when you are running out of time on your last question at the end of the examination time.

Use summary sheets for final revision of each subject and associated theories to aid storage and retrieval of main points. This level of preparation will keep the mind uncluttered before and during the examination.

Confidence in tackling the examination process builds from having knowledge of self and subject, belief in self and subject and above all the ability to put this knowledge and belief into practice within the set examination processes.

At college it's not enough to produce by rote if good marks are to be attained. Similarly, marks can't be awarded for strong argument and critical thinking in a subject area totally unrelated to that under examination. So reading the question and reading it several times is a must. Likewise the instruction within the question must be observed. Lack of recognition of the key issues and instructions within the questions is a major contributor to doing poorly at examinations.

You must remember that when the examination paper is presented to you, you start with *zero* marks but receive credit for every piece of *relevant* information that you provide in your answer. The examiner wants to find out what you know not what you don't know. You must also remember that the examination is not about the other candidates, it is all about you.

Poor presentation of work can lead to poor overall results. Sloppy work, squashed tightly together also makes the examiner's job very difficult. Leave lots of blank space between questions and between sections. Allow yourself space to return to questions to add in information if inspiration comes at a later stage, that way you have a stronger chance of leaving a legible trail behind.

Learn to manage time. Be clear on how long you have, how many questions need to be answered and how best to divide your time. Study previous examination papers, the number of questions asked and decide on a typical time allocation in relation to the marks awarded for each question. Why give half the time to a question which can only gain one third of the marks? This model can be applied to every examination question.

Ask yourself:

> What is being examined?
> How can I best prepare?
> What do I need to bring with me?
> When and at what time is it taking place?
> How do I get there?

> Do I need to pay a visit to the venue beforehand to check things out?

Never depend on word of mouth for location of venues, examination dates or examination results. Seek this information out for yourself, always. Colleges insist that it is your responsibility to find out the place, date and time of all examinations.

On the day of the examination
Arrive on time fully equipped. Bring your student identity card with you together with any other documentation as requested by college. Breathe deeply and take your time. It is unwise to engage in idle chat about possible questions immediately before the examination. This can be off-putting especially when some bright spark begins to expound on theories that you have never heard of and have the resulting effect of freezing your thought process.

Start with the topic you know and like best. This will free up the brain cells and give you confidence to tackle the remaining questions. Very often the number of questions to answer in a given examination can be few but the level of discussion required in some subjects can be quite significant. In this case, time passes very quickly and you may be left with a full question to complete as that final bell rings. Check the clock frequently. Time should be allocated proportionately to the level of marks awarded to each question and to each section within a question.

If time is running out and you have one remaining question, leave the question you are answering and immediately tackle the remaining question working in a focused manner listing the key and relevant points in bullet form.

Sometimes students take the 'becoming personal' route; "I can't answer this - I'm going to fail." If this happens to you, take a few deep breaths, steady the nerves, throw the issue out to the middle of the table and reverse the thinking to "I can and I will." A simple brainstorming exercise on the subject in question might put some direction on an answer for you. Think on your feet:

> › What am I being asked to write about?
> › Underline key words, the answer is in the question, so read it, read it again and again.

You need to work hard at the examination. You need to tell the examiner what you know about the subject relevant to the question being answered. Leaving early is never a good idea as inspiration on the bus home won't contribute anything to the situation.

Engaging in post mortems immediately after the examination is never a good idea. No two students will approach a paper in an identical manner. Trust in yourself, you are your own best critic. Post mortems often end up in frustration and tears which dilutes your confidence and ability to continue with your plans in preparing for the next examination. So the best advice here is to ignore your neighbour both during and after the process.

Unwell at formal examinations
If you are unwell and unfit to sit an official examination you must notify the college at the very earliest opportunity both orally and *in writing* and produce medical certification as evidence of your illness which clearly states that you are in an unfit state to sit the examination.

Where a student is deemed to be medically unfit to sit any examination and this is supported by medical evidence, a second opportunity may be afforded to that student to sit this examination, as a first sitting, at another time.

Where a student insists on sitting the examination in spite of medical advice and unfitness to do same, the student takes this risk upon himself/herself. In this situation, the college offices should be advised of the situation at the earliest possible opportunity and *in writing*, supported by medical evidence. However, in this case, the college will generally deem this sitting as a first sitting and the examination will be marked accordingly.

If you have a prolonged absence from college during the course of the year which negatively affects your academic performance, it is your responsibility to notify the college *in writing*, once this is known, and well in advance of the examination dates. It is in your best academic interest to keep college updated and informed at the earliest possible opportunity.

Check your course/college handbook/s for rules relating to all of the above.

Grading structures
The grading structures may vary slightly from college to college within the third level system. You will need to check the grading system in your college, however, the following may be taken as an example of how this can be broadly categorised:

Classification	Grade	Percentage
First class	I/A	70 - 100 %
Second class (upper)	II.I/B	60 - 69%
Second class (lower)	II.II/C	50 - 59 %
Pass (Some colleges award a Third class grade)	P/III	45 - 49%
Pass	P	40 - 44%
Fail	F	39% and below

To achieve 70% or higher at college, you need to be at the top of your game. Only a very small number of students achieve these high grades. Sometimes students coming from high predictive grades at second level find the level of marking somewhat penal at third level. They find that moving from achieving consistent A or B grades to a lower second class honours or even a pass grade inexplicable.

On careful examination of the criteria set for grading of the examination, the student learns to understand that critical thinking with well supported argument is rewarded at third level rather than the regurgitation of key facts from a very broad but not necessarily deep base.

Pass grades vary from course to course and college to college. On many courses the pass rate is set at 40% but on some it is set at 50% or higher.

It is vital that you check what pass grade applies to both your continuous assessment and formal examinations and how grades are classified on your course.

The alarm clock
If you live at home you may have an inbuilt security when it comes to making the examination destination on time, on the right date and of course at the right place. On the other hand, if you live away from home you may be totally reliant on the properly charged mobile phone to wake you without many of the home comforts such as a hot shower, a breakfast or a reassuring word going out the door.

Regardless of where you live, you must take full responsibility for getting there in good time. Chapter 8, Living at home or away, looks at the various challenges in both scenarios.

The next chapter looks at what is available in terms of college supports and services and how the awareness of these services can serve to optimise your academic and social development during your first year at college.

Chapter 7

MAKING USE OF COLLEGE SERVICES

Every college provides a unique set of services and supports for all students attending. These services may be called different names and grouped into different orders and dealt with by different offices at each of the colleges.

Colleges seek to provide services at many levels, all with the common goals of maximising your social, personal and academic development.

It is important that on entering the system you become familiar with all the services on offer within the college of your choice as the time will come when you may need some help or advice. Seeking help is seen as a wise and forward thinking move. Everyone needs help at some point in some aspect of daily life. The first step is in identifying what help is required.

The range of support services available can include:

›   Accommodation
›   Academic services
›   Careers services
›   Chaplaincy
›   Class Representatives
›   Counselling services
›   Disability services
›   Health services
›   Support centres
›   Tutoring/Mentoring/Student Advisory services

Accommodation
College provides assistance to students who are in search of accommodation both on and off campus. Campus accommodation, where available, is limited and should be applied for months in

advance of entry to the college. Please check the accommodation section on your chosen college website for these dates.

The accommodation office retains lists of various accommodation options which are regularly updated. Relating matters will be dealt with in greater detail in chapter 8, Living at home or away.

Academic services
A range of free academic and associated services is available to assist you throughout the college experience such as:

› Writing skills
› Study skills
› Library skills
› Research skills
› Referencing skills
› Critical thinking skills
› Life and time management
› Presentation skills
› Stress management
› Studying in groups
› Teambuilding skills
› Examination preparation

The development of these skills will greatly enhance your ability to perform and gain confidence in approaching the challenging learning situations ahead. These skills are also invaluable during work placements in industry while at college and later on when entering the workplace as graduates.

It is most important for you to identify areas where you might like or need to seek help and how to make the most of the available services. These areas will change over the course of your study path.

Careers services
The careers service office in college offers students advice on career planning, job searching, CV preparation, interview preparation and

practice, preparation for assessments and for multiple interview stages. This advice may be offered at group workshops or by individual arrangement.

This office works with prospective employers locally, nationally and internationally and acts as a central point for recruitment of graduates within the college. Employers are happy to interact with students at regular intervals through:

> Recruitment fairs
> Poster events
> Prize-givings
> Guest lectures
> Seminars
> Workshops
> Showcases of student work

The office also liaises with graduates who often return to share their experiences and offer advice on career paths to students.

If workshops are made available to you, it is wise to attend as many as possible. Given our current high unemployment rates, you must seek to perfect your CV, excel at interview and understand how best to fit with employers' needs both as a student and a graduate.

Chaplaincy
Colleges offer chaplaincy services which seek to support all faiths within the college community. Chaplains offer spiritual guidance to those who look for it and very often run seminars on related topics to which you will be invited to attend. Other social gatherings are also organised such as coffee mornings, lunches, parties, prayer sessions and interfaith gatherings. The chaplains may also offer confidential advice and guidance on many social, personal and academic matters.

Class Representatives

Every core course group in college will have a Class Rep, a service for students run by students and supported by college. The election of these representatives is often directed via the Students' Union. Class Reps are elected by their class peers in the course of the first few weeks in the first semester.

Class Reps are not elected because of their popularity but more because of their desire and ability to understand how college works, to see things objectively, to actively listen, to work well with others, to voice the opinion of their class and to act in a responsible manner in representing these opinions to college staff and officers. While the position carries academic responsibilities, the Class Reps are usually highly involved in organising many social activities for the class. They also sit on various committees and councils and can have the ability to influence policy at senior level.

Handling difficult situations at college can, at times, prove to be awkward business. If you find that you are having an academic problem, you can start by approaching the individual lecturer or course director or you can use the available college tutoring/student advisory/counselling services. However, you may feel uncomfortable about doing this on your own for a variety of reasons.

Class Reps can be most useful when it comes to students handling difficult situations or making complaints about matters that might arise over the course of their study. Complaints at college are often best voiced as one. Where there is valid ground for a particular complaint regarding academic or administrative matters, it can be best to seek a group or class opinion on the arising issues. Where a general consensus of opinion emerges relating to such complaints, the Class Rep can then become the voice for such complaints working on behalf of the group/class with course coordinators/course directors/lecturers/college offices/college committees and others concerned. While resolutions are not always immediately forthcoming, such efforts are taken seriously by college and course committees.

Counselling services

A free and confidential counselling service is available to you at college. This is particularly important if you run into academic or personal difficulties and need a helping hand.

These issues may present as a defined personal problem or may be the result of other influencing factors in your environment such as family sickness, bereavement or a very untimely departure of a good friend, classmate or family member.

Scheduled talks on managing many of these issues also take place over the course of the academic year. These might typically include:

> Mental health
> Suicide
> Drugs and addiction
> Money problems
> Eating disorders
> Depression
> Relationship problems
> Personal safety
> Dealing with anxiety, loss or grief

You need to stay tuned into notices about the general talks available which might help in a time of crisis. It is important to seek help early on with any problem you may be having as this will limit any negative impact on your ability to partake in academic and social activities while at college.

Disability services

Students with disabilities are well catered for at third level and there is usually one dedicated office which is responsible for giving this support. In the course of the CAO application, students may disclose any known disabilities. Guidance counsellors will offer advice in this matter. Information relating to a disability disclosed through the CAO should automatically transfer to new college records. Occasionally this transfer of information may get delayed or even lost in the process, so it is important to establish if the college has been notified.

If you wish to avail of disability services and you are unsure if your chosen college is aware of your circumstances, you must make yourself known to the office concerned.

Students with disabilities or specific learning difficulties may be eligible to apply for college entry under the Disability Access Route to Education (DARE).

Health services

Colleges offer a confidential medical service to all their registered students. Consultations are made by appointment and are offered at reduced rates. Some colleges may offer a limited range of free services.

The health services promote healthy lifestyle habits and work closely with the counselling services offering advice on the physical, psychological and social aspects of student health. Information is also widely available in many areas including: sexual health matters, nutrition, travel and vaccination, drugs and alcohol.

Many colleges also offer other medical services at reduced rates.

Emergencies always receive priority treatment.

Support centres
Most colleges run support centres to help students in certain areas within their particular course of study. These centres can provide assistance in many subjects such as: Mathematics, Science, Computer Programming and Languages.

Many colleges operate learning centres which can incorporate all of these supports. Information regarding the use of Information Technology services and equipment is also provided.

You need to establish from the outset what support services may be available to you in your chosen course of study.

Tutoring/Mentoring/Student Advisory services
All colleges have some form of confidential tutoring/mentoring/ student advisory system in place which is primarily there to provide support for all students. This is of particular importance for you to know as you as you make the transition from second level to third level.

These advisors are there to provide you with direction on any matters relating to practical, personal and/or social issues of concern. Such advisors are sufficiently experienced to direct you to the appropriate administrative, academic or support service. Often a short meeting solves the problem in hand and can save you a lot of time and effort in the end. This system can be the first point of contact, however, you are also free to make direct contact with the offices providing the services.

If you have a concern, at any time, which is affecting your personal, social or academic development, try to seek out the help of the many professionals providing these services. It is important to remember that a problem shared can be a problem halved.

Over the course of your time at college, it might be useful to conduct the following exercise in the context of the services on offer to you and your own strengths, weaknesses and needs.

Here's what I'm happy with	Here's what I may need help with	What service can help me?

The next chapter looks at the practical issues of living at home or away.

Chapter 8

LIVING AT HOME OR AWAY

Home is home. It's the sum of many things:

› The creaking step on the stairs
› The old sofa to lounge in
› The key that needs tweaking in the door
› A cuppa at the kitchen table
› The family gatherings

Every student has a different experience.

Home can provide a scaffolding of safety, rules and order and maybe sometimes the added bonuses of cooking and laundry and the comforts of light and heat without the responsibility for paying the bills.

Living at home
If you live close enough to your college of choice, then it would seem to be a wise economic decision to continue to do so over your time in college. This being the case, the relationship at home will need some review:

› How do you manage to have peace and harmony and live a student life at home?
› What position do you come in the family? If you have younger siblings you may be looked on to set an example.
› What are your expectations?
› Have you given any thought to what expectations your parents might have?

If you plan to socialise late at night during the week, how are you going to overcome the problem of coming in at all hours of the night and waking half the household up? What contribution are you planning to make towards the domestic running of the household?

As outlined in an earlier chapter this does not always have to be financial.

I am referring to the way in which you manage the space you live in, how you keep that space and how you expect others in the household to fit in with your management style. It may be perfectly acceptable to you to let laundry pile up in several bundles distributed unevenly across the bedroom floor or to expect that a shared bathroom might be devoted solely to your use and the availability of hot water to the family dependent on how long you sing in the shower.

› Does any of this sound familiar?

Until you are paying the going rate for renting a room, you have to make efforts to cooperate with those who pay the mortgage or the rent and the many bills associated with the running of a household.

Safety issues can be a big concern within any household. As a matter of courtesy, it is usual practice for family members to give a rough idea of their whereabouts to avoid unnecessary worry and to make provision for meals.

Your parents will naturally worry about your whereabouts and wellbeing. It takes considerable adjustment of the mind-set to shake the shackles of 18 years of knowing your daily schedule to an open and unaccountable style of movement. Add to that the issues surrounding the consumption of alcohol, often at inappropriate and unplanned occasions, and communications can become fraught and difficult to manage at home.

You can often feel homesick while living at home. Sounds strange, but this homesickness arises from the changing relationship between you and your parent, the loss of the old school relationship and the social difficulties presented as you begin a new and at times challenging journey of change. Probably for the first time since birth, you will make new friends without any influences from a familiar network. Joining societies and clubs at college is a good way to deal with this homesickness.

I'm not sure just how nature intended adults to live together at home in harmony. One thing sure is that every adult has his/her own expectation of how to do this. It is also important to note that men and women can approach this process quite differently.

Living away from home
Those who live considerable distances from home will have to find accommodation close to college. This is a very expensive process and many things need to be considered. Have you thought about where you might live?

Campus accommodation, where available, is set aside specifically for the use of the students at a particular college and can be located on the college site or off site. Costs will be identified up front whether on or off site and may include bills for utilities and other services. If the campus accommodation is located away from the college site, it can often be within walking or cycling distance, however, it may also necessitate the use of public transport which will add to the already high accommodation costs.

College campus accommodation is limited to small numbers so if you are planning to go down this route, this needs to be checked out months ahead of entry to the system.

You will be asked to pay a deposit on booking the accommodation and following your course offer, payment of the relevant costs will be required. Where there is a sharing of facilities, you may have little or no say about who you share with. Policies differ from college to college.

Once you sign up to taking campus accommodation, you will be given a strict set of rules to which you are expected to adhere. If you break these rules, you are bound by the disciplinary rules of the college and the disciplinary committee will decide what penalties can and will be imposed.

In these circumstances, you may risk being asked to leave your accommodation and such an early departure may also attract a large fine and forfeit payments made to date. If you are expelled from college for any other reason, then you will also be asked to leave the accommodation and may be liable to pay the full year's costs. The system can be more or less penal depending on the case in question and the rules applying within each individual college.

Read all contracts carefully before taking up any offers of accommodation and the payment of any deposits, fees or utility charges.

Living at home or away: Health and safety issues
It is not the purpose of this book to pass moral judgement on any student activities but it could be fair to say that there is national concern relating to the overall consumption of alcohol among young people in Ireland today. There is also concern regarding the misuse of prescribed drugs and over-the-counter medications, and the use of illegal drugs. Students need to become more informed about the effects of all. Advice is available through the college health/counselling services.

From a health perspective it is important for all, regardless of age, to look after the body. The sports analogy is useful here in the context of alcohol consumption. If we go through hours of physical training and don't feed the body afterwards, the body suffers. Likewise if we fail to feed the body before large quantities of alcohol are consumed, then we can equally neglect the body. Given the intoxicating effects of excessive alcohol intake and the resulting often most unacceptable behaviours, it is wise to adopt the policy of eating before drinking. If you form this habit at a younger age, then this practice will remain with you for life.

Unfortunately, some students find themselves at the centre of negative encounters that can attract the eye of the law. Such encounters are almost always associated with excessive alcohol intake. When you are over 18, it is important that you understand you are no longer a minor and should charges be brought against you and you appear before a judge in court, the family account of your good behaviour holds little value. Should this happen to you, your criminal record may be about to begin. Such records will determine your freedom to work and travel overseas and in many cases will preclude you from holding positions within government office or the teaching and caring professions, to mention just a few.

Other safety issues relate to the physical whereabouts of students, particularly late at night. Our daily news updates remind us of how being in the wrong place at the wrong time can happen to anyone. However, it is wise to take some precautions such as staying in groups, avoiding making unnecessary journeys alone late at night, avoiding darkly lit places and staying out of geographical areas which are unknown or known for the wrong reasons.

Almost all colleges offer student health and counselling services which provide information regarding healthy living including: mental health, physical wellbeing and sexual health. Students can seek advice on all these matters through this service.

Living off campus in standard rented accommodation

If you choose to live independently from the college, then you will be looking on the open market for a place to rent. The accommodation service in college may be able to assist with advice on the best places to start the search. Given that the academic year usually spreads over nine months, students often end up paying higher rents as landlords make the case that they cannot occupy the properties for the remaining three months of the rental period.

Rents for accommodation situated within walking distances of most colleges will usually be more expensive, however, living close to college eliminates the need for public transport costs.

Many factors must be considered prior to entering into a rental agreement which can include:

> Proximity to college
> Public transport costs
> Safety of location
> Safety of overall neighbourhood
> Security of the house
> Proximity to shops or supermarkets
> Typical utility costs
> Type and method of heating
> Cooking facilities
> If timer devices are fitted for water and heat

Public transport costs will have significant impact on all budgets.

You must read the terms of any rental agreement with care. If the agreement states there are to be no house parties, then the landlord has every right to evict the tenant if the agreement is broken. Landlords do not want and will not tolerate hassle from students. Pleading ignorance of this fact falls on deaf ears. Respect your neighbours, they are only an arm's reach away from a telephone and will not hesitate in contacting the authorities to bring order.

House sharing is great when it works. The freedom of living and managing your own space can be a liberating experience. It can be such fun. However, the old saying "if you want to know me, come and live with me" often brings its own troubles and very soon irritating habits can cause untold friction within a shared space, so much so that living at home suddenly becomes quite an attractive proposition!

Some students are comfortable from the outset with their fellow housemates and may even know them quite well and know exactly what to expect. However, in some cases students take up the individual renting of rooms without knowing anything about their new housemates. This can be a little daunting.

Some students, under pressure from home, may be persuaded to live in a family home or 'digs' during the first year at college. The student will be bound by a certain code of conduct which is usually explained by the household at the outset. It works well if the home is warm and welcoming and good facilities are offered to the student. This is not always the case and quite often students end up in unsuitable accommodation and find it hard to express their dissatisfaction as they feel that they are locked into an arrangement at enormous cost to their families.

Cooking
Regardless of where you live, students are expected to work within a set tight budget. If you don't know how to cook, it's time to learn to do so. Try experimenting with a half dozen eggs, a kilo or two of mincemeat, lots of tomatoes, a bag of unwashed potatoes and a large packet of pasta to see how it can stretch to feed many and still provide some choice on the menu.

This is so important when it comes to living in rented accommodation. Where there is cooperation, the cooking of communal meals can work well, particular with the lads who, it has to be said, are less fussy than the ladies!

You must also learn how to cook all in one pot or at a stretch using two as, even in this 21ˢᵗ century, cooking facilities are often limited to two rings and an oven which doesn't work. You need to be creative in the kitchen and with your money. Good planning saves euros. Off the cuff spending in the local convenience store on the way home from a gig in college can blow one week's budget in an evening.

Homesickness affects many students living away from home and particularly so at weekends. If this happens to you it is so important that you use every opportunity possible to become involved in social activities and attend gatherings on campus. Some students look for part-time work but this may be unavailable and not a good fit with overall academic demands. Others look to engage in charity/ volunteering work and there is plenty of this to be found at any time of the day or night and over the weekends if it is sought out.

Living away from home outside the country
If you plan to live away over the summer months, the same rules relating to looking for accommodation apply. If you head for sunnier climates it is important to note that air-conditioning bills can be like heating bills at home and there may also be other hidden charges, such as water and refuse.

As already pointed out, it is of vital importance to ensure that you at least explore the matter of health insurance cover *before* leaving the country, regardless of duration or geographical location. If you require hospitalisation and you are not covered by insurance, it is hospital policy in many countries not to release the patient until the bills are paid, in full. Prepare for such an eventuality, it is a small price to pay in the overall context of travelling for a summer or even a year abroad.

Again remember to carefully read and understand all rent agreements prior to signing. This applies worldwide.

We now move to the next chapter and back to the more academic functions of college life and what it takes to become a successful student.

Chapter 9

BECOMING A SUCCESSFUL STUDENT

The answer to becoming a successful student lies with you learning to manage the learning process. Much mention has been given to the art of independent learning throughout this book and this chapter will seek to help you develop skills in adopting this art.

Success is about setting and achieving goals. Goals need to be clear, and practical, have clearly defined steps which are set within a realistic timeframe.

Clear
Your goal is about a target you want to achieve:

> Is it that you want to learn music or that you specifically want to learn to play the piano?

Realistic
> Is this possible for you to achieve? You have 12 weeks to do this.
> What can you realistically expect to learn in 12 weeks?

Practical
> Do you have the necessary tools and time to achieve your goal?
> Do you have a teacher and is there a cost factor involved?
> Do you have access to a piano on a daily basis for practice?
> Are you willing to set aside at least one hour every day for this purpose?
> What exactly can you achieve within the allocated time?

Clearly defined steps
> Break down the steps to manageable daily and weekly tasks that are not too daunting
> Check your progress regularly

Identify your goal	*Place a time limit*	*Outline steps to reach goal*	*Review - check your progress*	*Reward your efforts*

For every goal achieved, it is important to treat yourself with some form of reward. Reward takes many shapes and sizes and can be little or large. The personal satisfaction achieved in the accomplishment of a defined target or goal may be enough reward in itself for many.

Take responsibility
This starts with finding out what your day demands in terms of attendance at lectures, tutorials, demonstrations, study and other as outlined in chapter 4, Day to day life at college.

Seek out key information
You need to seek out key information relating to all subjects and courses of study including:

› Deadlines
› Key dates and times
› Examination structures and associated rules and regulations

These are all discussed in the chapters dealing with the handbooks and the examination process.

Believe in your own ability

You have come this far, why not go further? Success is unique to each and every one of us. It is in these differences that we celebrate. If you believe in yourself and your own ability to perform and make the effort, it will be rewarded.

Become an active learner

You need to drive the learning process and become a self-directed and independent learner. Part with negativity, leave it outside the room. Adopt positive people into your company. If you hang around with moaners, then you will become one of them. Get rid of excuses such as: 'if only...'

Take Control

›   Use I statements.
›   I can, I must and I will
›   Accept that it is you that has to do the work

Explore

You need to consistently question, seek out new opinions and new directions and new ways of doing things. The successful student is open, sceptical not cynical, enquiring but not arrogant, and respects the views of others.

Deliberately learn

You need to have purpose attached to every formal learning time. We learn in everything that we do but as we begin to work at a set time in a particular space we deliberately embrace the art of learning.

›   What do you want to achieve during a particular learning session?

Manage time

There are 86,400 seconds in a day:

›   On average we sleep for 28,800 seconds

> What do you do with the remaining 57,600 seconds?

Everyone needs to sleep, eat, study, work, meet with family/friends and pursue leisure activities.

> Have you thought about how you balance your time?

Common timewasters include:

> Being disorganised
> Working in cluttered spaces
> Moving from task to task without completion of any
> Putting things off
> Spending too much time on social media
> Dealing with interruptions
> Constant crisis management
> Being a perfectionist in all activities
> Losing things
> Making excuses

Can you examine how you approach tasks in light of all of the above?

You can also lose a lot of time travelling to and from your place of study. Use this time to plan, read, revise or listen to relevant material.

Make the best use of lecture time
Prepare where possible for your lectures. If you can, read in advance and question what you need to know. Whether using pen or keyboard you need to be organised to get the most out of this time. Date every lecture, giving each one a new page/section. Develop your own shorthand code.

Identify verbal signposts that you may pick up from your lecturer indicating the importance and relevance of the subject under discussion. Note why these points are important and when they might be most useful. Almost every lecture will have a simple structure of a beginning, middle and an end. It is also equally important to read up on the topics covered at the lecture as quickly as possible afterwards.

Making good use of notes

Your notes are your own personal guide to study and should be rewritten soon after the individual lecture. This will aid memory, retention and retrieval. Your notes should reflect a summary of the lectures attended and link with other lectures following in the same subject area.

It is essential to file these notes in a systematic order in clear divisions from other subjects. This is such a worthwhile exercise and a practice that will stand to you for life. It is also important to establish if there are supports that you might seek out to enhance your understanding of the subject area such as: library, labs, tutorials, seminars, study group meetings and other college supports.

Electronic files should be backed up at all times. Email or cloud computing solutions are useful in this regard, however, it is also advisable to save your work to a portable hardware device such as an external hard drive or USB key.

Getting down to the business of study

The obvious questions include:

> Where can you study best – at college, at home, at your rented accommodation or other places?
> When is the best time for you to study? Is it late at night, early in the morning, at set times during the day or different times every day?
> How much time works for you to study best? Are your efforts wasted after a number of minutes or are you effective over longer periods?

No one size fits all. However, if you study over long periods, it is wise to break after 40/ 50 minutes to walk around, stretch the legs or take a glass of water. It is important to have a question set out to answer for each study period as it gives a focus to the learning.

Like all goals achieved, be kind to yourself with a treat when you have been effective during your study time.

Group work

Students often work together in groups to maximise study opportunities and share information and opinions. Students bring their own strengths and weaknesses to the table, some obvious and some not so obvious.

Groups provide natural avenues to discuss assignments, difficult subject matters within the course, approaches to work and the introduction of new academic resources. Where groups are imposed on students, problems can arise mainly due to underperformance which has already been dealt with in chapter 4, Day to day life at college.

If group work becomes an integral part of your study process, then it must be carefully managed.

Thinking critically

› Do you actively seek information and do you seek validation for this information?

› Do you accept what you read or do you seek out the opinions of others?

In academic terms think about the following statement:

Global warming is a myth.

Think about what reasons might contribute to such a statement. Seek academic evidence to support or refute this statement and work towards reaching a position where you are capable of critically discussing and analysing both opinions. Now the critical thinking cap is on.

Examination technique

The examination process has been addressed in great detail in chapter 6.

Try and find the techniques that work best for you. Particular attention is required to develop memory skills by experimenting with different ways of storing and most importantly retrieving information under pressure. Examinations are solo runs, you are there on your own and everyone works differently under these conditions.

To be a successful student you need to believe in yourself, see the challenges as opportunities, take ownership and responsibility, be organised and disciplined, be clear in your goals, monitor your progress, seek feedback and reward yourself when the work is done.

The final chapter of this book, Where to from here, gives some practical tips on starting out.

Chapter 10

WHERE TO FROM HERE?

This book set out to inform students and parents about making a smooth transition from second level to third level and making the most of that first year college experience. Some insights have been offered on choosing the right course, academic matters, getting to know the third level systems and the services, the art of independent learning and the many challenges of living life at home or away

In chapter 1, Setting the scene, I began with the parent perspective. In this, the final chapter, I will begin with the student perspective.

The Student perspective

Mobility, employability and active citizenship are key to your success and contribution to the world we live in. It is in this context that we need to understand that you are being educated for a world of change, that jobs for life are things of the past and much of the future depends on creativity, innovation and entrepreneurship. Given the unpredictable nature of the workplace today, it is difficult to foresee many of the jobs of the future.

Follow your own dream. Therein lies the key to your opportunities. Find something that you like to study, that you want to study. Embrace every learning opportunity and every service that can enhance that opportunity. Visit the college campus of your choice and explore all contact opportunities. Become well informed before making any decisions.

Regardless of your involvement in sport and community activity at second level, seek to develop your interests, other interests and widen your circle of friends by joining college clubs and societies.

Know what you are good at and identify what you need help with. Nobody is perfect at everything. If you have a natural flair for languages, work on them as they are key to mobility and employability worldwide. Where support centres run specific courses or drop in clinics to assist with any of your subjects, avail of them. They are run for a reason.

Build your own set of unique skills and try to do something new every semester or at least every academic year. Keep this practice with you for life, whether learning to cook, paint or take photographs. It's good for the soul.

At college, make every effort to attend registrations, orientations, lectures, tutorials, laboratories and demonstrations and try to use the many supports and services available to you. Develop your network and get to know the campus and the systems. Understand the importance of the gatekeepers of the college, the administrative staff who liaise with the academics, those who take in assignments, those through whom you have to work to gain access to study rooms, those who hold the keys to buildings.

Be prepared to work hard at getting the best out of group and team situations. Be prepared, visible and vocal at tutorials. Don't waste time. Be clever in your approach to study and if you have part-time work, make it work for you, not the other way round.

Fitness and diet are all important. You have one body, so treat it with respect. Remember when you are over 18, you can't be defended as a minor in a court of law.

Think about how you communicate with others. Exercise good manners; be pleasant and greet people as you pass. The simple words of 'Please', 'Thank you' and 'I'm sorry' go a long way. Be kind to others, you will reap the reward many times over, maybe not today or tomorrow but in time to come.

Take ownership and responsibility for all that you do. It is your future. It is your destiny, it is all yours.

Try to let go of your worry, your woes and any unsettled business of the past. Whether this is with family, friend or foe, it's time to let go and start afresh. There will be tough times ahead but remember that there is always help and support available. Don't look back, tomorrow is always a new day.

The Parent perspective

It is a difficult time for parents, as they try to let go yet guide you in your preparation for an unpredictable world of work in a time of great social and economic change. So what can they do to help you face the challenges ahead?

They can support you through all the examination processes on the road to third level. If you are in the middle of the first year college experience, you also need support, perhaps in not such an obvious way. Parents need to understand what is normal behaviour for you and seek advice should they see any abnormal patterns emerging. They need to encourage ownership and independence in all aspects of your life.

Chapter 3 referred to the biggest challenge for parents as being that of listening and supporting without interfering. This challenge still stands.

Parents will have their own expectations. After all, the educational experience to date has been facilitated by them and it is my guess that many of them are getting ready to facilitate this experience for a while longer.

Parents are now entering a new chapter in life's cycle. The handholding is over and it's time for a few serious ground rules to be set. The conversation about finances must take place and the implications regarding living at home and away need to be spelled out. This conversation is likely to be repeated. Such dialogue can also have a very maturing and positive effect on this changing relationship.

It is only right that issues around health and safety are also discussed. I think it is also fair for parents to expect that you will make every effort to use the college services and supports available to you and attend the various registration and orientation meetings, induction sessions, lectures, tutorials, laboratories and demonstrations/other. It is reasonable that they should expect you to be proactive in college and make a genuine effort with study. If living at home, some house rules need to be agreed to. Rules were made to be broken so parents need to remember to think carefully and have few!

Finally...

I return to the first line under the heading 'The student perspective' in chapter 1:

You, the student are the most important person in this book. This still holds.

College is an adventure, a preparation for life, personally, socially and professionally. It is a privilege, not to be wasted. It is a once off opportunity to invest in your development in a recognised, organised and secure academic environment. It's a time to read widely, to learn that learning is a continuous development, to become informed, to develop ideas, values and opinions and to become contributing, mobile and employable citizens of our world.

Be safe, have fun, keep well.

Strive to be happy.

Useful Links

Association for Higher Education Access and Disability (AHEAD)
AHEAD is an independent non-profit organisation working to promote full access to and participation in further and higher education for students with disabilities and to enhance their employment prospects on graduation.
www.ahead.ie

Central Applications Office (CAO)
The Central Applications Office is a not-for-profit company which was founded by higher education institutions (HEIs) to process applications for entry to HEIs in the Republic of Ireland centrally and to deal with them fairly and efficiently. The HEIs retain the function of making policy decisions on admissions.
www.cao.ie

Career Directions
Career Directions is a careers matching programme that provides career ideas and information together with career options. It incorporates an 'Interest Inventory' which assists the user in identifying work preferences based on likes and dislikes and presents the user with a range of suitable careers that best match their preferences.
www.careerdirections.ie

Careers Portal
CareersPortal provides a comprehensive source of careers information in Ireland. Designed for people exploring their career and educational options, it brings together a vast range of essential up-to-date information on courses, careers, job opportunities, labour market trends and careers news. It contains dedicated sections for school and college students, adults and parents.
www.careersportal.ie

Central Statistics Office
This Office serves the needs of the wider national and international community (media, researchers, students, businesses, representative organisations, the EU, international organisations, and the public generally) for impartial and relevant information on social and economic conditions. Particular attention is paid to the specialist needs of business and the research/academic community for more detailed and focused data.
www.cso.ie

Citizens Information
This site provides comprehensive information on public services and on the entitlements of citizens in Ireland.
www.citizensinformation.ie

Department of Education and Skills
The Department of Education and Skills has responsibility for education and training in the Irish state. The mission of the Department is to provide high-quality education, which will enable individuals to achieve their full potential and to participate fully as members of society, and contribute to Ireland's social, cultural and economic development.
www.education.ie

Disability Access Route to Education (DARE)
DARE is a college and university admissions scheme which offers places on a reduced points basis to school leavers under 23 years old with disabilities who have completed an Irish Leaving Certificate.
www.accesscollege.ie/dare

Higher Education Access Route (HEAR)
HEAR is a college and university admissions scheme which offers places at reduced points to school leavers from socio-economically disadvantaged backgrounds.
www.accesscollege.ie/hear

Higher Education Authority

The Higher Education Authority is the statutory body established to allocate public funding to Irish higher education institutions; to oversee performance of the higher education and research sector generally and to advise the Minister for Education and Skills on the development of the sector.
www.hea.ie

Institute of Guidance Counsellors

The Institute of Guidance Counsellors is the professional body representing over 1200 practitioners in second level schools, third level colleges, adult guidance services, private practice and in other settings.

On behalf of its members and their clients the Institute has a liaison and advocacy role with government departments, management and trade union organisations, national parent bodies, higher and further education institutions, employment and training agencies.
www.igc.ie

Mocks.ie

Mocks.ie provides a service for students from first year to Leaving Certificate which includes: revision notes, mock oral exams, mock exam papers and solutions, mock aurals, multiple choice questions, correction and feedback service and career guidance.
www.mocks.ie

National Centre for Guidance in Education

The National Centre for Guidance in Education is an agency of the Department of Education and Skills, with responsibility to support and develop guidance practice in all areas of education and to inform the policy of the Department in the field of guidance.
www.ncge.ie

National Consumer Agency

The National Consumer Agency (NCA) has a section especially designed for students going to college. It includes information on finding somewhere to live, student banking, budgeting, paying bills and money saving tips. They also have a section for students to compare bank accounts, loans and credit cards on their financial product comparison page.

www.nca.ie/nca/going-to-college

National Parents Council Post Primary

The National Parents Council Post Primary (NPCpp) is the voice and advocate for parents and guardians of young people in post-primary education and is the umbrella group for secondary parent associations within the Irish education system which includes: Co-operation of Minority Religions & Protestant Parents Association (COMPASS), The National Congress of Catholic Schools Parent Associations (CSPA), Federation of Parent Councils in Christian Brothers & other Catholic Secondary School (FEDCBS), The Parents Association for Vocational Schools and Community Colleges (NPAVSCC) and Parents' Associations of Community & Comprehensive Schools (PACCS).

Working with these associations and in consultation with government offices and agencies the NPCpp offers co-ordinated training, interaction, information and engagement with parents and guardians on current and emerging issues. It provides a forum that actively supports parents and guardians in their parenting role and interacts with schools and other education partners on issues that impact on the education development and general well-being of young people within the post-primary education system.

www.npcpp.ie

Qualifax

Qualifax is Ireland's National Learners' Database. It provides comprehensive information on further and higher education and training courses. Qualifax has developed services so that students can make informed choices about their education, training and

career paths. It includes a range of useful tools such as an events calendar, interest assessment and points calculator.
www.qualifax.ie

Quality and Qualifications Ireland
Quality and Qualifications Ireland is an amalgamation of four bodies: the Further Education and Training Awards Council (FETAC), the Higher Education and Training Awards Council (HETAC), the National Qualifications Authority of Ireland (NQAI) and the Irish Universities Quality Board (IUQB). It is the agency responsible for the National Framework of Qualifications and the quality assurance of further and higher education and training (including English language provision) in Ireland.
www.qqi.ie

Student Finance
This is a useful source of information on financial supports available for further and higher education. It also provides a useful links section incorporating the National Consumer Agency, already referenced in this section.

The Student Grant section provides a comprehensive source of information on available schemes. It provides information on course fees and on eligibility requirements for free fees and other sources of assistance for students, such as the Fund for Students with Disabilities, the Back to Education Allowance and the Student Assistance Fund.
www.studentfinance.ie

UCAS
Universities & Colleges Admissions Service, UK
This is the UK equivalent of cao.ie
www.ucas.com

***

Colleges in Ireland

Universities

Dublin City University	www.dcu.ie
National University of Ireland, Galway	www.nuig.ie
National University of Ireland, Maynooth	www.nuim.ie
Trinity College Dublin	www.tcd.ie
University College Cork	www.ucc.ie
University College Dublin	www.ucd.ie
University of Limerick	www.ul.ie

Institutes of Technology

Athlone Institute of Technology	www.ait.ie
Cork Institute of Technology	www.cit.ie
Dun Laoghaire Institute of Art, Design and Technology	www.iadt.ie
Dublin Institute of Technology	www.dit.ie
Dundalk Institute of Technology	www.dkit.ie
Galway-Mayo Institute of Technology	www.gmit.ie
Institute of Technology, Blanchardstown	www.itb.ie
Institute of Technology, Carlow	www.itcarlow.ie
Institute of Technology, Sligo	www.itsligo.ie
Institute of Technology, Tallaght	www.ittallaght.ie
Institute of Technology, Tralee	www.itt.ie
Letterkenny Institute of Technology	www.lyit.ie
Limerick Institute of Technology	www.lit.ie
Waterford Institute of Technology	www.wit.ie

Teacher Education Colleges

Church of Ireland College of Education	www.cice.ie
Coláiste Mhuire, Marino, Dublin	www.mie.ie
Froebel College of Education, Dublin	www.froebel.ie
Mary Immaculate College, Limerick	www.mic.ul.ie
Mater Dei Institute of Education, Dublin	www.materdei.ie
St. Angela's College, Sligo	www.stangelas.com
St. Patrick's College, Drumcondra, Dublin	www.spd.dcu.ie

Other Colleges

All Hallows College	www.allhallows.ie
American College	www.amcd.ie
College of Computer Training	www.cct.ie
Dublin Business School and DBS school of Arts	www.dbs.ie
Grafton College of Management sciences	www.graftoncollege.ie
Griffith College Dublin	www.gcd.ie
ICD Business School	www.icd.ie
Independent Colleges, Dublin	www.independentcolleges.ie
Irish College of Humanities and Applied Sciences	www.ichas.ie
National College of Art and Design, Dublin	www.ncad.ie
National College of Ireland, Dublin	www.ncirl.ie
Pontifical University of Maynooth	www.maynoothcollege.ie
Portobello Institute	www.portobelloinstitute.ie
Royal College of Surgeons in Ireland (RCSI)	www.rcsi.ie
Shannon College of Hotel Management	www.shannoncollege.com
St Patrick's College,Thurles	www.stpats.ie
Tipperary Institute	www.tippinst.ie

***

Universities in Northern Ireland
The Queen's University of Belfast

Queen's University Belfast	www.qub.ie
St Mary's University College	www.stmarys-belfast.ac.uk
Stranmillis University College	www.stran.ac.uk

The University of Ulster

Belfast	www.ulster.ac.uk
Coleraine	www.ulster.ac.uk/campus/coleraine
Magee College	www.ulster.ac.uk/campus/magee
Jordanstown	www.ulster.ac.uk/campus/jordanstown

***